Nellie's

Kids

To my Mam, no longer with us, yet we are never without her.

To my beloved wife and kids who never disbelieve in me.

To Liza for the fantastic cover art & Sign Geer Ltd for the graphics.

To my patient beta test readers, my select friends who helped me formulate my ramblings into a coherence.

Thank you all.

DISCLAIMER

This is a work of fiction. Names, characters, business, events and incidents are the products of the author's imagination. **Any resemblance to actual persons**, living or dead, or actual events is purely coincidental.

PUBLISHING DETAILS

Publisher: Independent Publishing Network

Publication: July 2023

ISBN:978-1-80352-860-1

Author: Raghnall Cagney
Email: rtcagney@gmail.com

Please direct all enquiries to the author

PROLOGUE

My earliest memories of this special place do perhaps come
with the benefit of a handsome amount of hindsight. But
they form a solid clue towards who I would become.

You see I have three clear memories of this, my first place
of refuge. It was a humble home in middle class 70's
Ireland. It stood there, a semi d, amongst the many others
about it. Red brick on bottom, white paint on top, the sills,
and plinths, a dark strong black. Some had a metal black
pull up garage door. Others an extra room for use as a
'good' room or a dining or a hobby room, possibly. They
all had foot-high timber rail fences, interrupted by a
driveway where some of the others had a lawn.

By these clumsy, first introductory words, you are now
possibly assuming I'm an estate agent, about to describe
floor types and views and such, and that is not at all the
correct direction in which to go. You see the clue is not so
much the place, more so the events that took place, in the
address (it's somehow corny, to have said place there
again; but seems less cheesy to mention it now, within

these brackets.) It was here, that I came to understand, was my first home. Therefore, it is absolutely the locus appropriate to the commencement of my story.

These events were 1) Summer 1976. As a tiny baby, my mum proudly, on one of those rarest of things, a sunny day, left me soaking up the rays in the garden cosily from my shiny new pram. As an addendum to this highlight of my life it has to be said, that this was during the hottest summer in Ireland on record, for a long time. The heat then not such a luxury and a little dangerous to my one-year-old baby soft outer layers. A fact a wise and interfering (and I would say old, but of course, I was less than a year on earth, at the time) neighbour, pointed out to my doting mum, with a firm rebuke to bring him, that is me, indoors. Yes, my mum thinking she was doing the best for me nearly microwaved me! But she did so from the best perspective of all, a new mum who wanted the child to be happy and content in the sun. Some would argue on this and preach from a pulpit to my adult self, that this was bad parenting and should not have been remembered fondly. In fact, this was normal behaviour then. It was common enough to hear of fellas, who were moisturised in olive oil to encourage a tan. Today they have the tan and are in no way resentful that they were essentially deep fried on the sunnier days of their lives.

2) Dry day in 1979. I aged four, was in a toy army jeep cart type thing in the back garden with my dad posing beside me. Smiles and banter abounded, a totally nice image of suburban life in Mr Haughey's Ireland.

The clue as to my career is this, these memories are of course manufactured. I'm not denying they're real, they did happen, but I don't actually recall them. The story was told to me by my family, much later on. I can visualise it in every detail, but I don't remember it, not really! The jeep thing I have a picture of. Not just a mental one, but an actual polaroid. We both smiled for the camera. I can remember many exchanges with my dad, just not this particular one. Manufacturing stories to satisfy my purposes has gone on to become a useful tool for my trade.

3) Eviction Day 1982. Like a lot of people, my family found the 80's a difficult time financially. I found out as a seven-year-old that no money meant no house, security, or refuge. Only the well-endowed could have such things.

I still remember sitting in the back of my mums brown Fiat 127 watching the court appointed removal crew throwing our stuff into the garden. My dad loading a borrowed Hi-Ace van with the big stuff. A particularly cruel bailiff type, saying to my mum, if she needed a bed for a night or two, he'd sort her out, not dad and I… just her. She did not seem impressed with his offer. He leaned into her to say his cruel jibes to intimidate her. I was too small to offer any meaningful defence. I remember the jumped-up twerp reminded me of a dog. He had a mark like a black spot below his left eye. It was like a spot on a canine. But this guy was not man's best friend. His mumblings to mam really upset her. Only natural when you consider the ongoing trauma of the eviction.

Mum cried. Dad was quiet, too quiet but I took his cue and quietly stared at the bad people taking away my idealism through the 127-rear windscreen, as we drove away. Had I spoke up in fairness, I'm sure they'd have told me not to worry, that I was too young to understand. They may have then said, "but I will."

This was real, in no way a manufactured memory and so it gave me a fire in my belly, to become a have, as opposed to a have not. On that day, subconsciously I was imprinted by the school of hard knocks, to be a man of means, by any means possible. I have always thought myself, to have a decent moral compass. But stood on only so many times, you will be, before you will feel a primal inclination to fight back! I had seen my parents struggle with being in penury. That would not be my fate.

BEGINNINGS

The hostile takeover of our home then became the normal way of Banks administering pain and suffering nationwide. Some of those affected, organised a form of resistance. They picketed the banks and their own homes. They crashed in and disrupted auctions. The banks continued repossessing homes, with their sheriffs backed up by Gardai for moral support. They had the power to smash through front doors and forcibly remove people. At least they acted as they had. The Irish people had no chance as they lacked organisation to effectively fight back. Many dreamed of a fight back worthy of Michael Davitt's Land League. Few delivered it. I wanted revenge and would happily as I grew up, talk rubbish about banks and bankers.

My mum and dad rented a series of small homes, moving about a bit doing various jobs to stay alive. They worked hard at shop keeping jobs, in hotels and nightclubs, got me educated and died happy and satisfied as a result. I have to acknowledge here the cruelty of life. Mam died in 2011 of being worn out by life and its harshness aged seventy years. Dad had died in 2009 after years of being a shouldering support to mam of bowel cancer that spread aged sixty-six. (Mental note to self. I must visit the graves. It's been a while.) The devoted pairing had tough lives, but they had succeeded in weaving a rope for me to cling to. (An occasional visit to tidy the graves was the least I could do.)

Their final venture was really for me, the most important one. They got a good old Credit Union loan and bought a barn on a rural road in Co. Tipperary. Put a huge sign outside it, Bargain Buys call 0504-33257 DEALS!! The phone number easy to remember, just dial the word Deals and hey presto, 33257! People came in sound numbers and bought and sold to us. I learnt the rudimentary parts to negotiation and closing a deal. It does not matter in fact how you are trying to make a living; you simply need to understand people and what makes them tick.

Understanding human nature, you could normally get people to pay a bit more for your tat. Yes, basically manipulate them into it. The key being, make them believe they *want* your tat. Good luck with that. But we did. Or rather THEY did. I simply watched and learned. And my parents did this well and gifted me that self-same ability, to seal a deal, which I could rely on many times. For them it meant, their end was more secure than their beginning or middle. Realised in the form of them being able to buy a beautiful 1940's house, complete with its own (now sadly filled in and closed up for safety) air raid shelter. A cool novelty none the less. It was a cold house with steel single glazed windows, but they warmed it with love. Then they even upgraded the windows. As with most parents, mine wanted me to have the best they could manage. Given earlier upheavals, this was a source of pride. This house and the atmosphere within, were evidence of the triumph of the human spirit, the instinct for survival. Most satisfying for them was the fact that they bought the house in a depressed time, therefore at an affordable price, from a downsizing bank manager. Not the one who ousted them originally and I'm sure the trade down, was a practical solution to the problem of age, as opposed to an economic necessity. Yet it was sufficient for them. Not for me, my disgust for bankers and the establishment was becoming fever pitch. I was radicalised to hate them. Nights out drinking, would be spent concocting ways of removing their capitalist yoke of oppression, with likeminded drinkers. Alcohol loosens inhibitions, many ideas were considered. To me, my drinking buddies were serious sounding boards for my revenge planning. To most of them, I was just an entertaining drunk, who they should humour as after all, I shortened their evenings.

Growing up I also learned of myself, that I loved a thrill, to live on the edge. This again would be an essential skill of a con artist in the making. A school sports day was looming. The main event, a football game of teachers vs. students. A bit of banter with my accountancy teacher and voila, I'd taken a bet from him that the teachers would win. I offered the three to one odds. He staked a tenner. A lot of money to poor student me, even in 1991, as a fifth year. I could just about cope with that, but next thing I knew, half my year had bet on either teachers or students to win. I knew nothing about how to run a book. One of my fellow students, asking to place a bet, saw a panicked look on my face. "You are out of your depth," he said. He even gestured the universally recognisable sign of water rising above head. I agreed and that's when I met the first of my crew recruits, Timmy McGuire. He tweaked my odds as new bets came in and engineered a break even, regardless of result. As it happens it was a draw, but I had not specified a draw meant no pay out. I was happy, even though I had to refund all investors. You see, we did it. It was the first time we pretended to be what we were not and got away with it. It felt flaming good. So, from then on, we looked for ways to recapture the buzz.

This ultimately involved becoming scam artists. By the way as I'm going to some lengths to tell you this story I may as well tell you my name, Jack Delaney, charmed to meet you and at your service.

A PLEASANT DAY IN THE COUNTRY
1960

Nellie was at home that day helping with chores. It was
only a small holding. But dishes needed washing, clothes
airing, and potatoes needed peeling. Her mammy was a real
worker, but help was welcome. It provided a fine
opportunity to assess her daughter's domesticity, a skill
which would increase her marriage prospects no end. It also
allowed for seriously enjoyable mother-daughter quality
time. Nellie had a funny bone on her, she was one to laugh
and provide laughter in their home.

Her current joke de jour was something she had read, in a
magazine, ordered by the local doctor's surgery for the
purpose of distracting the patients in his waiting room. He
of course, often read the material first. Had read it since he
was a boy, in fact, as it sat on his father's waiting room
table. Of course, he was allowed then by a father, who
valued his love of reading and now by virtue of the fact that
he paid for the annual subscription to the Readers Digest.
The doctor was a kind man, but he might not take kindly to
knowing his edition of the magazine was practically second

hand. Nellie would have voraciously read the thing cover to cover, by the time he collected it. This meant, she would have the jokes off to share with... whoever was listening.

Oh yeah, joke de jour, "The one good thing about a colour television! When someone on Bonanza gets called a yellow belly. You can now look to verify."

This was funny to Nellie regardless, but television was new to Ireland even in black and white. So, it sounded sophisticated as a joke and Nellie liked that too.

The cottage half door was already letting in a bit of light and noise from the farmyard. The girls heard the men coming across from the distance. They could hear the duck, the geese, and the pig scratching around the place, grunting, honking, and quacking, happily. Nellie adjusted her hair. So vain and yet so innocent and unaware of why she acted like this, when he was about.

Her dad came in, pushing aside the bottom half door as he did. In followed young Johnny Murphy himself. His tweed coat still carrying bits of straw, from the time in the shed. He had been there holding a bull bar on the hinds of a lively one. She needed some veterinarian potion that she would not welcome. Johnny Murphy had volunteered to help Nellie's dad in a kind of Health and Safety capacity before Health and Safety was ever a thing.

"A cuppa, now Johnny lad. You've earned it." said the grateful father. He continued, "Nellie a square of butter too, with the brack."

"Ok Da, I'm on it!"

"And turn that noise off," said dad referring to the radio, which was playing Good Luck Charm, a recent Elvis number one.

(A good time to bring up an idea I have. As I write this book, I'm dreaming of seeing it in film/movie form. A pipe dream, I know but why not play along. Post me on the platform X, formerly known as Twitter, @nellieskids1 with your soundtrack suggestions.)

She blushed thinking, "dad shut up," and turned it down. A perfectly lovely afternoon tea transpired. Johnny was grateful. Time elapsed quickly into the early evening when

Johnny announced he had to be off to run another errand for another neighbour. This encapsulated life in Ireland, at the time. The good bits. You see Ireland, in the sixties, was still a largely rural community. People came together to get tasks done. Saving crops and it's like, was far easier when numbers of farmers came together to work and so they helped each other. The Cooperative movement now maybe eighty years old, was becoming popular in Ireland. As modern Ireland was emerging with its urban and industrial bias, it was so important, that the rural folk clubbed together. Many of the smaller farmers could not afford the big machines and so a pool of labour was just about the only efficiency they could achieve. Johnny Murphy was a good citizen in this regard, always willing to help the local farmers when he wasn't working above at the stud.

Nellie asked the parents if she could walk out with Johnny, as his route would take him past their orchard. Her plan was to return with enough cookers to undertake a tart for the Sunday dinner. Her father and mother both had a sweet tooth and thought any plan culminating in an apple homemade tart was a really good idea.

The two innocents went for the walk. The gorse was in a subdued, even wilting bloom, clusters of green and yellow limping out of the hedges as their seasons peak was passing. The birdsong lilted in wisps of air passing them overhead. The sedge warblers are preparing to sing their way back to Africa.

He listened to her recalling the contents of the current digest, from the ant's organisational capacity to the jokes at the back. She was unstoppable, even if he wanted to. She was nervous and so seemed to be talking more. He just liked listening to her. And then before either of them realised they wanted a kiss, they arrived at the orchard. "I better get these apples picked. It will be dark soon. Off with ye!" Johnny smiled at her and took to nibbling on the straw he was still finding on his jacket. He turned and strode away. Nellie started giggling to herself, jumping from tree to tree with a song in her heart. The basket was full in no time. She was light on her feet, even with the heavy basket to haul home. These apples were the first fruits of what was normally a decent haul of fruit. On her return, she entered the kitchen, singing. Well, it was more of a hum, with an occasional word sang. Mam and Dad sitting at the table drinking more tea; smiled knowingly at each other.

"What are ye two, grinning at?" said Nellie, a little irritated to be stopped from the humming.

"Nothing shur," Dad replied.

Mum supported him with, "Aye nothing at all."

"Will you stop it so?" Nellie said laughing with them now. She was happy, they were happy.

"I'm off to bed. I'll be up early to make those tarts!"

"Night love." The contented parents called after her. "Sleep well."

On the stairs she passed the window giving a full-on view of the setting sun. She sprang upstairs and into her room, closing the door behind her. She picked up a pillow, hugged it like a child's comfort blanket and daydreamed of him happily: until the nineteen-year-old fell asleep and probably dreamed of him then too.

THE MARK
2023

If Jack Delaney was going to retire it made sense that the last big score was also going to totally make a fool of and therefore hurt the one-man Jack has always hated. Mr Aidan Cohen, C.E.O. of Nova International Investment Bank. It was nothing to do with his current job as a banking supremo although it would have been enough given his honed hatred of them. But it was for a more specific reason than that. It was because he was the bailiff on that day. If you asked Jack as to why him, he would simply say, pacing back and forth as he did so, "He was there, he may well have been just a cog of the wheel, but he was there. This miserable toad, this reptilian, this chewer of the cud was there."

It wasn't some bailiff; no, it was this miserable excuse for a canine lookalike who insulted Jack's mother on that fateful day. He went on and on about how they failed everybody as parents; because they couldn't keep the roof over their heads and how he would move on, sell the house, leaving them with nothing as they deserved. They may well have recovered a bit in the finish, but not Jack. He hurt for them and had planned his revenge ever since.

Some might say, you can't cheat the innocent. Some bleeding hearts may start thinking he had a job to do, that Jack's parents should have been aware that their home was, as the ad says, "at risk if they did not keep up the payments." Jack would from his bias never look at the mark as innocent. That said we're not in Hollywood now, there's no one not con-able. Innocence is actually irrelevant. Some are more satisfying marks that's all. Aidan Cohen was for sure.

As a child Jack had no clue who was who on that day. The enormity of it all left him hating the bankers passionately but as an anonymous group. Subconsciously, he would always be able to pick out the dog impersonator and so he did. Fast forward a few years to when he was a man in most senses of the word. A garage forecourt. He paid for his fuel but on the way back to his car, he clocks him. A breeze chills the air. The guy getting into the back of the Mercedes had the spot birth mark. Can it be him?

All the memories of the frightened little boy peering over the fabric seats and out the back window come back and surrounded him like the breeze. Jack noted his registration like a proper gumshoe, in one of those tiny black flip notebooks with accompanying pencil normally held in place by a strip of elastic. He then went and did some research, his due diligence and discovered .... well, he can at last, get him!

How? He planned to use Cohen's greed against him to give him an offer he could not refuse.

Jack Delaney's research said of Aidan Cohen that he was first and foremost a journey man. Yes, he had achieved success and made it to the management level of the finance company he works with. But from what Jack could workout he had done so by being just that bit more anonymous than his colleagues. A finance house requires that its staff would maintain a good reputation, publicly at least. Some of Cohen's associates failed to do this in certain cases. It was because they had personal indiscretions which, when made public, called into question their sense of moral uprightness, forcing in effect their retirements. It was all quite exciting, some of the stories involved their financial indiscretions, but others were carnal. Whatever got the job done! Trade journalists would speculate if Mister Cohen had anything to do with the revealing of the secrets but the journalist who published them never confirmed their suspicions. Jack had no trouble in believing Aidan Cohen capable of fabricating these stories, of being a backstabber to friend and foe. So much so that, as last man standing, he was able, through a management buyout scheme to become the owner of Nova. It was all his.

In truth the concept of being journey men though, was something the two enemies, even if the hatred was at this time one way in direction, now had in common. Delaney never aspired to be the best. This sting would simply make him that. It was just an accidental coincidence, however. Jack, starting out before that meet at the petrol pumps simply wanted to survive, to maintain the buzz given by successfully pulling off a scam. In a way to remain anonymous. It's been said that the secret of being a good cleaner is that no one notices you. They don't see the space get dirty, your cleaning, nothing for them changes, you stay anonymous. The same is true in con artistry. Being anonymous to marks as well as the authorities is the goal. Going unnoticed whilst criminal investigators are nipping

away at those who dare to be noticed is the ideal. Ego
makes you want to be noticed. This was where Cohen's
weakness began. Jack was happy to remain hidden, a
journey man till the bitter end. Aidan Cohen was starting to
like the attention. Ego makes you overachieve and that gets
you caught. That's true in business too. Think of the recent
banking and financial scandals in Ireland. These institutions
had become too big, so their mistakes were harder to
recover from. They therefore fell notoriously, as opposed
to, in memory of the good they achieved, on the way. They
were no longer journey men but players in disgrace. Instead
of the numerous homes and other assets built, bought and
insured by them; instead of the intangible societal good
achieved via locally directed sponsorship, all anyone now
talks of is the greed that brought them down.

In sport the concept illustrates well also. Delaney loved two
sports, soccer and snooker. His team Norwich nicknamed
the Canaries had in the twenty years he'd followed them
been up and down from the premier league, a lot. So much
so he called them the yo-yos. But without them and
another dozen similar teams the top eight could not
function.

The same is true in snooker. The big nine or ten names need the other hundred to exist to make the competition circuit work. The headlines are always grabbed by the top few. The remainder happily anonymous.

The only question then that remained was which journey man had the biggest ego? Who would lose this battle due to his own hubris? Cohen or Delaney?

SHE

1950

She awoke from her slumber as people around her came to
life also. The train was pulling into the terminal at
Kingsbridge Station. The carriage was full of people
preparing to alight from the wheeled cannister and so,
provided her rude awakening from zzzz-land. As she
climbed out of the train, she heard the engine still
ruminating. The cacophony was completed by the clatter of
rain on the tin roof overhead, along with the melodious
accompaniment of an occasional whistle, from a ticket
inspector. She was pushed along the platform, which was
funneling everybody to the more expansive lobby at the top
of the terminal. Once there, she was able to stand
motionless with her bag by her side in the big city. She
looked up at the high moldings on the lobby walls. How
grand! How sophisticated! She was a city girl now.
Although the country version of herself, fought away its
extinction by causing her to notice the skinny silvery
painted lattices of iron holding the roof up and observing
rhetorically that they reminded her of frozen spiders' webs

that were common enough in corners at home at this time
of year.

Getting herself together she walked out in an amble looking
for a bus or taxi to her digs. Others were also employed in
finishing their journeys. For instance, a group of hob-nailed
boots with carpet coats. The type worn by many a
utilitarian worker with the leather patches just to the front
of the shoulder. All cocooned in tabards of the C.I.E., dark
orange red colour were heading for home. She discerned
this by the way they were swinging their now empty lunch
boxes, laughing at one another's jokes.

In the wintery failing light of the dreary November
evening, she was happy to find the rain had stopped since
she got off the train. The taxi rank with 3 cars parked and
ready. "Where to luv?" enquired one of the cabbies in a
cheerful Northside accent, as he climbed off the foot board
of a neighboring cab whose driver was chatting with him
from within. She handed him the address prewritten on a
piece of paper. For her the journey was not near its
termination. She was having belly butterflies precisely
because her journey was only just beginning.

**(How about SHE by Charles Aznavour for the
soundtrack, your choices remember to @nellieskids1. I
really will enjoy reading them. For instance, my son just
recommended to me from "She's" point of view, Jonah
Kagen's Broken playing whilst She is on the train….
thinking things over. Then he came up with Dermot
Kennedy's Heartless as from the absent loves point of
view and that put Good Thing by Fine Young Cannibals
into my head. Look at me getting carried away. A great
game to play along to!)**

Her thoughts too had never been far away from he who was
the cause of her relocation. Would time away make things
easier or would absence make the heart grow fonder? Time
will tell.

1961

She clumsily alighted the train on to the platform. Her
rotundness was not yet noticeable but sufficient to make
movement uncomfortable. She looked up to the blank wall
where one of the new trendy advertising companies was
erecting a billboard. These new-fangled marketers were a
nod towards the country's modernisation. Of course, many
other signs of this fact would follow. For instance, all the

old place names of the English would be dumped in 66, that is 50 years after 1916. So, Knightsbridge would become Heuston Station. She didn't discern these momentous changes in the offing or indeed muse upon the social consequences of such change, but it would come. Unaware, she simply imagined the new advert hoarding as a score board for country people to tick when they arrived. A tick on the left for a good reason to visit or on the right for a bad reason. She imagined every year; little Christmas brought the rurally based shoppers. Otherwise, it was probably a medically necessitated trip. And they are nearly never good. Moving out to the taxi rank she wondered which way she should be ticking life's imaginary scoreboard. Left or right, good, or bad.

(Let's use She again for the soundtrack. This time the Elvis Costello version to emphasise the passing of time.)

TEAM BUILDING

2023

Jack tried to achieve this type of invisibility a lá the previously mentioned journey man, in his work too. So, looking around his office surrounding the important white board where he laid out a scam, you'd see a pretty normal office. There is a desk for every member of his core crew and Jack himself. Pot plants etc. dotted about. It looked like a normal office. In fact, it was a normal office for the legitimate cover business in the warehouse selling the Deals. It was a huge part of how the crew stayed under the radar. This meant one member of the crew had that one job, doing all the normal and legal paperwork for real. In this office if an outsider entered, he was Jack's chief administrator, although they all knew Delaney was the owner. The shop staff would report to him when Jack was absent, which was often. It had to be Timmy as Jack's No 2, given he had shown from the start that he was good with numbers. In handling the office, he had to spend a lot of time at a computer and therefore he handled the I.T. end of things as well. He was crucial to bringing a result therefore in this final score.

Anyhow, it was from this office that marks and intended targets were identified, discussed, and researched. The crew had weekly meetings outlining the various current operational status of ongoing projects. They would debate solutions to problems as they arose. In this respect they were identical to any other business. Any casual passerby would easily be fooled into assuming they were a regular office doing regular office things. They even brought in packed lunches which when busy they ate at their desk. When not, they'd eat in a huddle where they'd discuss Norwich FC, Snooker, GAA, Politics, what's on TV and all the other water cooler stuff, normal office people discuss.

Timmy occupied the second desk. He was often called on by whoever was running the scam to do a fake web site or other fake records. It was now so easy to create an alternate universe and present it as a reality in a convincing way as the ploy of the day demanded. Sometimes this was a one-off situation where the carcass of the dead scam would then be abandoned digitally so none would ever trace them back to Jack, Timmy or the other crew members. Other electronic deceptions were on going and in need of maintenance, again in exactly the same way as with legit commercial efforts.

For example, one of the main projects Timmy managed for the crew was an insurance brokerage website. This was a constant money spinner and needed his regular attention. He was forever adding patches to the underpinning I.T. framework program running the scam. This was so it stayed running, taking in money but if anyone looked, they would have to follow the trail of so many proxy servers and shell companies, no one would ever connect it to the Tipperary boys in their little office.

The website looks real enough. It asked you to put in your details like it cared about your age, address, years with no claims etc. Then gave you a quote, one of three, 1299, 654, or 339 euros. These figures were picked as they read as forensically selected numbers by the actuaries of the insurance company involved. The customer however was just getting them sent out randomly. Jack could not afford an actuary and as it was not a legal enterprise, he didn't require one anyway. They were encouraged to pay by card, but the I.T. always knew if you were a debit or credit card customer and actually crashed on debit transactions. A customer would get annoyed and look elsewhere. The ones paying by credit card would go through, but only at the 339 rate so if ever discovered the card company would refund the client with no fuss. The crew had affected basic policies with genuine companies but would mock-up the paperwork, using these for multiple customers so many careful drivers who were fortunate enough to never meet a routine traffic stop, would never even realise they had been scammed and were not in fact insured. This was a genuinely easy thing to do. A simple web page with a big glossy of a smiling family stood around a car. Many immigrants had arrived in Ireland and looked for cheaper than the normal insurances. The gap in their English meant the website was never scrutinised hard enough for signs of fraud. Timmy was constantly changing the brokerage name or graphics or contact details. His job was to continually represent the fiction, factually so that no one would ever get close to the fraudsters whilst the monies involved would flow seamlessly but invisibly straight to them.

Timmy would play a large part of the final blow out scam on N.I.I.B. (Nova International Investment Bank.) I.T. support would always be crucial on a banking scam. As with all his team Jack never questioned McGuire's loyalty. He could be trusted and was carefully selected as a result. Whilst Jack had received McGuire's help in those halcyon days of schoolboy bookmaking, Timmy had got it back in return. As adult (debatable point admittedly) drinking buddies Timmy confided in Jack.

"I got a bit of bother with a bookie." The irony was beautiful. Jack's turn to return the favour. He did but not before he got every conceivable laugh out the situation on pub confession night. Even Timmy was laughing at the stupidity of the thing by the nights end. They both would have hangovers to remember…and/or forget, depending on your point of view.

Forty thousand was not so huge a figure that a proper solution could not be found. But the bookie seemed in a hurry and was threatening violence. Jack came up with an imaginative way to get the debt cancelled.

Compromising photos of the married bookie were delivered to him discreetly. The accompanying notes highlighted that his wife would be able to insist on a high financial price for his infidelity. The fact that Jack's female crew member was the scantily clad temptress Mary Jean or MJ for short, was never discussed...

Entrapment or not, grudgingly he wrote off Maguires' debt.

He'd always been grateful to Jack since, hence his loyal soldiership. He had become an electronic gladiator for the crew. Timmy, as of the above, would also be there for MJ if ever she found herself with bookie's remorse.

MJ too, she had her reasons for wanting to support Jack, in his endeavours. As a young one, she ran from home which was a violent place. MJ had been free loading around Ireland till he caught her pilfering at Deals. He said he'd call the cops (an empty threat if ever there was one) or she could work for him honestly. So now she was front of house at the warehouse shop.

From that, over the years she dabbled with his con artist life too, as his beautiful assistant. Although Jack was asking her to use her charms in predictable ways, he never put her in a dangerous situation. He knew the wrong mark would trigger the upheaval of her past within her. Helping get Timmy free of the bookie was probably the only time he put her in a bad spot. It was her melt down at operations end that informed him and Timothy of her fragility and its cause. Both men became very protective of her, from then on.

It would seem Jack's band of merry (wo) men was beginning to take its shape.

ANCIENT HISTORY
1962

Nellie Madigan was a joyous soul. This was in keeping with the fact that she was born in 1941. So yes, she lived through the war, but was far too young to remember any negatives. The war was over. Optimism was the only way. Now we were barely in the swinging sixties, but everybody was eager to get on with them. Her parents had endeavored to provide her with a non-worried life. The farm could not earn enough to keep them. So as soon as Nellie was of working age, she was put into it. She had no resentment; this was simply how it had to be.

Her current job was as a shop assistant in the local village shop. A fine emporium of its time. It was here she gained access to her stealthily read Reader's Digest. If so inclined, you could purchase anything from a nail and much bigger items of hardware (although normally that was sold by Philly, the man in the shop) to grocery items or a bit of haberdashery. Knickers were sourced there by some farm spouses. She could find much fun in her interactions with the local community during the day.

Men came in throughout the day. Some would be after tobacco. But some of the younger ones were in, really to chat with her. Johnny Murphy was a good example of that.

In fact, the gaggle of women who came by, at the same time of day, usually for the harmless gossip, if not for the groceries; they maintained him to be a fine specimen, that Nellie should watch herself with that one!

But now her shift was over. It was gone past four o'clock. And she had about a quarter of a mile done on her route home when the rain started to spit softly.

It was a lovely summery day, thus far. This precipitation was completely unexpected. So of course, Nellie had no coat to protect her from the changing conditions. A Land Rover pulled up alongside her. It was brand new. Its owner was obviously in the assent in life. It was Mick "Horse" Flanagan. His farm was next along the lane from Nellie's. He had to lean forward to lower his head so Nellie could get a clear view of him asking, telling her really, "I'll give you a lift, girl." She hesitated but only briefly. The shower escalated itself. The innocent gratefully got into the jeep.

Angry was the sound of the engine as it pulled away precious cargo aboard.

Nellie complimented the driver on the new jeep. Privately she thought now he needed to learn how to drive it. It was as if he was aiming for the potholes. Was it his way of showing off the jeep? Whatever the reason, she, a slight slip of a thing was being bounced about more than she liked. She showed no displeasure though, as she did not want to be ungrateful for the shelter offered from the rain.

D-DAY
2023

You can earmark a special day to execute an operation. To everybody else it would be just a regular day. Desiree Moloney leaving for work, for example. She was just a barmaid. Her job was repetitive and often meant listening to drivel from drunks. For this reason, she never really looked forward to work. She was very good at her job; she earned good tips. It put food on the table and provided her self-respect. She had therefore reason to carry her head high as she headed for the bus to work. She just never quite did. Her job was one of spurted exuberance. Sometimes the thought of it was really quiet exhausting. She found herself leaning on the bus shelter. Subconsciously, she rubbed her belly along the scar line.

Tamsin Clark was a busy mum. Her day was going to be city centre shopping. Not the fun kind but "the got to get that" kind. She would have to bring baby. It was literally a coin flip for her on enjoying the day. Would baby cry in protest at being dragged about? Would the shopping bag split open at the wrong time? Would the rain fall on them as they moved from shop to shop? All a coin flip.

As she brought the buggy to the door, she had to pause and circumnavigate around it to get to the worn carpet portion where a few items of post were scattered on the tan acrylic surface. She picked up the exit obstacles, so tiny and yet immense enough to prevent the onward motion out the door. She glanced as she put them on the side table, tactically positioned to mind the post and keys and such. There was a phone bill, a flyer to the local electrical outlet and none of these held her interest, for now it was time to shop.

"Yes, little baby kins, mammy's going to the shops, and you are coming too.... yes, you are!"

Aidan Cohen had an energy about him. He pulled over to the kerb. Jumping out he reflected on how much wealthier today would ultimately make him. "Latte please," he said to the street vender. First, he had to deal with the cops snooping around his books. He was dishonest. They couldn't prove it. He'd be ok. He returned to the backseat of the Mercedes M Class and told the driver to be work bound. The Aussie complied without a word. Sitting in the back, he continued his train of thought. At sixty now he was still young and worth millions, his exacting dad and doting mum would have been proud. He would have loved to give back to them for helping him in life. But he only started seriously accruing wealth since the nineties after their passings in a horrible car crash. He resented their absence from his life. A speed bump jolted him back and he stared out at the streetscape for the journeys remainder.

The Simpson family were on day four of their seven-day blitz around Ireland. In a few short days, they'd be back on the metal bridge, awaiting to board for their home journey to England. In their car, listening to the radio, they were!

("Yes of course, that was the E, the L, and the O with their anthem, Mr. Blue Sky. A scarce commodity these days…or is it? News and weather next!")

(Soundtrack for sure!)

They were happily half listening to the radio and half dreamily anticipating their day ahead. Today a trip to the Rock of Cashel, the Swiss Cottage, and to Cahir Castle. It was going to be a cultural day, true enough. But that's no reason it could not be fun also. Grandad would be providing ice-cream and minerals and chips as required. Granny would want to see the shops, her research showed that towns like Thurles and Clonmel had some nice ladies boutiques. The grandkids along with her; although their taste was somewhat more street than granny could comprehend. This would cost grandad. That was the price of happiness.

They were on holidays after all. In truth, they had earned their holiday. By being busy in life, they were starting to fragment as a family, to grow apart. Their daughter had stayed at home as she could not get the time off work. Although having the evenings in peace was hopefully giving her a satisfying rest too. The antidote was found on the Discover Ireland website in the form of this 7-day break.

("In the news today, a con artist steals a car by impersonating a priest. For details let's go to our local reporter.")

Grandad Simpson loved history and had crammed a few
outings into this trip. It was really potluck as to whether
granny and /or the kids would enjoy those bits of the trip.
The last one would be good, the Titanic quarter. All that
talk of a sinking ship would get the kids in giddy form for
the ferry home from Belfast the next day.

What the Simpson family was not realising, of course, as
most of us don't, is that history is everywhere. It's all
around us, if only we knew it. Life would be so much more
interesting.

BRAKES ON!! Grandad Simpson stopped his car, with just
enough time, as a beach type ball with a normal football
hexagon pattern printed on it bounced across the road in
front of him.

As a little boy got back his ball, the family looked about the
quaint village. A typical country pub, church, shop
(newsagent) and small primary school all brightly colored
timber facades with names over their doors; except for the
church, grey, drab, austere. The fact that the church
dominated this little village streetscape was a fact in most,
if not all rural communities around Ireland. It was

emblematic of the immense power (now well waned) once held by the religious orders and institutions, in Ireland's now distancing but recent past.

Accident averted. The front seat passenger, she who must be listened to, piped up. "Ah luv, I see a shop there. I think we are ready for a lolly, eh?" Grandad dutifully pulled in and replied, as he looked longingly at the shop door, "off you go then." She jumped out of the car glad of the leg stretch. She was now of an age that it didn't pay to be sedentary for too long.

As she got to the door a card taped on its inside, to be visible outside, attracted her attention.

"The History of BallyGortMore. Scandal, Violence, Impropriety - Absolutely not a dry look at history. Walking tours every Wed or Sat 10.30 for ten euros each."

She looked at it, she gave serious thought. Nothing that outrageous could really happen in a quiet spot like this. Could it? Anyhow, it looked too dark for the kids. Maybe if they were not there, she might.... but they were, so no dice. It had to be lollies and onward Christian soldier.

They drove on in the family motor, passing the sign, "Thank you for visiting BallyGortMore." Just beyond that an articulated truck was pulling onto the road from, as the livery stated, Boswell International Haulage & Storage. Its livery was blue and gold on a white background. These were the county colours. He knew this as he had already seen an abundance of flags out in support of the team and had asked a local of their significance.

As a truck twitcher or spotter since he'd started following Eddie Stobart trucks around England at truck shows, he had no bother identifying the truck. It was the international truck of the year the MAN TGX. The livery also virtuously explained how the firm gave two per cent of its earnings to children's charities. Old man Simpson mused, "Does this company have a social conscience or is it a hyper cynical marketing ploy?" This machine was the business as trucks go, but not in its ideal environment of open road just yet. Its slow progression meant Grandad had to slow to a crawl again and so noted the mammoth operation. It had a large warehouse with forklifts and people moving about like ants. Chaos, it seemed and yet organised. Fancy trucks and a busy spot. They were doing well. The Simpson clan would probably be behind the thing now for ages. It was only a B road. "Bummer to be us," he thought. Still, he was on the hols, no need to rush, just enjoy the drive. Yeah!

Jack drove towards town (the city of Limerick) wondering why all culchies refer to cities as towns. It's part of that underdog mentality of all rural people he guessed, a belief that somehow they don't belong, have no right to experience the sophisticated urban sprawl that is city life. He called it the Wild West factor. Just as a cowboy in many old westerns went into town to conduct business and to get drunk, so too would many a culchie limit his visits to town to similar constraints. At least he had this morning and what a "today's business" it would be! The mere thought of the day ahead necessitated a mop of his brow.

He couldn't help thinking too, that those who knew him would probably regard him as a bit of a cowboy. In fact, they would probably regard him in much more negative and colorful ways. This stray thought chilled him a little. He never really liked to think of what other people thought of him. This shook him enough to focus his mind on the labour ahead.

Today was a big one! If he pulled it off retirement was the only option. At forty-eight, he figured he had enough excitement. Perhaps one of his young apprentices could take it over, although if today went well he wouldn't care as he'd have enough money to buy a little island paradise somewhere. Of course, it would be in the sun. He could never figure out why someone like Haughey would buy off the coast in Ireland. Where's the luxury there? No, it had to be somewhere sunny for him. His thoughts were clearly still straying a little as he approached the Newport roundabout. He decided to pull in and perhaps a quick cup of tea would settle him! Turning left for the appropriately named "Fill Up Again" bar car park he reflected that he always found it hard to concentrate, in fact he was quite a dreamer. This was why he'd been told in school by one of his teachers, "You're good for nothing and that's what you'll do... nothing!"

So far in life Jack Delaney had proved his teacher wrong. His living was at times luxurious but mostly comfortable. The fact that it was all completely illegal was hardly the point. After today, his old teacher would have the satisfaction of being right because if the scam went well, retirement followed. A lifetime of doing nothing!

He stepped out of the car, his own and not one of the many he'd "borrowed" in the course of his work. Work allowed him all kinds of cars as the job required. On his own time, he chose to drive a Toyota Avensis. Not flashy, just functional and yet it provided enough comfort to make most trips enjoyable. Perhaps more importantly it provided something very much desired by all well-adjusted con artists, anonymity! Drive anywhere he could and simply blend in. Many of his past scams (this was before he borrowed cars to suit the job) involved working crowds out shopping. In that situation his car looked like any of the other family saloon's taxiing granny, mammy and the three brats from shop to shop. In the more subtle business community type scam, the Avensis was camouflaged as sales rep saloon. Anonymity guaranteed.

Jack's nerves today were a little fraught. 'Twas not a lack of belief! Jack knew he was good at what he did. The size of this deal was the frightening part. This was worth fifty million euros, less his share of expenses. It was a lot of money for one deal, by most people's standards. Inside Fill Up Again, he hurriedly found a table and sat with coffee, muffin, and the business pages. He decided on coffee, as tea wasn't a strong stimulant to him. Although a whiskey bottle flirted with him, hanging upside down behind the bar, its glowing reddish-brown color inviting him to call for a measure. He declined, of course, as today a clear head would be required. He would make his way over to the international investment bank offices situated in Saint John's square in the city centre.

SHE, THEM AND HIM
1955

She really had to admit she loved the new version of herself. Coming to the big smoke from BallyGortMore, was quite possibly the best thing she had ever done. It allowed her to reinvent herself. She was no longer defined by her mistakes and her past. I know right, MISTAKE but it was a BIG ONE. Yes, he was.

Anyways, that was the past. The nervy little girl had arrived and convinced her employers to promote her out of probation and give her a shot. She was good at what she did. She was on a management track; richly deserved it too.

The only problem was with the actual job. It left a lot of time for solitary contemplation. Sometimes it was during times ring-fenced naturally for deep meditative thinking. Then during other less obvious times of the day, when she was supposed to be too busy to think, she still found time to remember inconveniently, what she wanted to forget.

She wanted to feel sorry for herself but couldn't. There was far more deserving of her pity around Dublin, and she threw herself into helping them at her work in any way she could. She just never forgot.

(Has to be Red Cortina by The Saw Doctors for soundtrack. "First love stays with you forever." A great line!)

BEST LAID PLANS
2023

As an example of perfect timing, his phone vibrated on the table, wobbling sufficiently to threaten falling to the floor. Seeing the screen illuminate prompted Jack to pick it up. He read it. As expected, it was Timmy.

"In position Jackie boy, how are you?" Those were the first words that Jack heard from the phone speaker. "Fine fettle, Mac, no complaints at all," he replied. Without waiting for a reply from Timmy, he continued, "Operations report, then?" McGuire was ready for the question, having the list to hand. Jack had the phone between his ear and shoulder in a pincer movement, so he could swallow some breakfast, while listening to "insurance brought in €1009.59, three stings yesterday." (This was the scam mentioned earlier). "Learning courses €1398, two stings yesterday." (This scam was mentioned on many websites, dash questions.ie for example, the discussion thread spanned two months and involved fifteen contributors. Although Jack and Timmy use different screen names to back their side of the debate, most of the comments were negative. This scam involved selling educational courses guaranteeing a professional support structure leading to the taking of recognised exams. The phone number supposedly provided support, instead of bringing frustration. But no one ever answered! On the upside, the course material was legitimate in its relevant field. The crew had bought them, the entire offering of legitimate online colleges on the dark web where someone quietly sold them after hacking the college main frame. The materials genuineness meant nothing if you didn't understand it, you were on your own.) "Clothes recycling, no figures yet but we filled the transit twice. I have a meeting for the trade." (People gave good quality clothes, far too good for throwing away. But who from a drought prone country would want a gray raincoat, complete with super comfy lining, anyway?)

Jack nearly choked on the coffee as he tried and eventually succeeded in replying, "You set a meet today! You're supposed to be backing me up, what if?" Timmy came back quickly with, "Don't go having a heart attack." He then went on to explain that his meeting was at the milk market car park just five minutes away within wire range. The traders could only meet today.... blah, blah, blah. The exchange carried on along these lines for a good minute or so before Jack decided to end it. He felt Timmy was letting down the operation, but forty-five minutes before a major sting was not the time for debate. Either way, later today he'll bring it up again and put Timmy right! For now, team morale was perhaps more important and so Jack could only muster the feeble comeback, "You better be there for me when I need you!" As he said that he gave a jabby first finger as if to tell off Timmy. "No sweat," came the reply. "By the way, have you got a car yet?" he further enquired. Jack concluded, "no but I'll make contact enroute. Let you know what I finish up with." Timmy was excited too for the day ahead. "Fair enough so let's go and make some money," he said.

It was now 9:47am. Jack knew he was prepared to be fashionably late if there was such a thing. But this was too close for comfort. To be excessively late could sour the mark and should therefore be avoided. He needed to get moving. Jack had decided to leave his own car at Fill Up Again. A borrowed car would be used from there on. If all went well, the car would be found later today and returned to the owner but if it went a little awry, the car having no connection to Jack might confuse anybody in the pursuit, for a while anyway. Jack got up to pay the bill and ironically in so doing felt a little conned himself for paying eight euro fifty for a black coffee and muffin (he recently had to pay ten euro fifty for four razor blades. He didn't enjoy being ripped off as he saw. He decided to buy an electric razor. Just because he'd earned it easy did not mean he had to lose it in the same way.) He quipped to the cashier, "I suppose it would have been nine euros if I'd had milk in the coffee." The cashier was not amused and launched into a counter tirade. His volley was shrugged off by Jack who was now headed for the entrance lobby. Once there he had to pass the reception desk again to whom he said courteously, "see you again." As he said this, no one looked up, they merely grunted and carried on working on the lunch menu. This meant no one noticed him grab a jacket from the coat rail. He literally whistled his way out of the door. Once outside he stopped whistling. His pace quickened into the car park as his hands fumbled through the pockets. When he found the keys, he threw the jacket into a nearby standalone plant pot.

Volkswagen keys, not bad, but which one, he thought? At first glance he noticed maybe five or six, all well-spaced out. Partly from time pressure, partly from adrenaline and partly from panic he decided to run about the car park pressing the remote locking button. Suddenly a silver Golf R32 standing three rows away, one car to the right beeped as its indicators flashed. In seconds, Jack was in the car, out of the car park and on the mobile. Exiting from the car park he turned to the left towards the city. His speed was of a man who knew only too well that this was not his car. This was his "hire" car. He would treat it as everybody treats a hire car, shamefully! The result was that on yanking the wheel left to pull into the traffic, he pressed hard on the aluminum looking foot pedals and his inside rear wheel lifted just enough for people to notice him. The noise from the highly polished chrome twin centre exhaust pipes ensuring the effect. He was noticed by a Mercedes driver, pulling in for a meeting with some fellow business acquaintances. Although after a bit of imbibing he couldn't be regarded as a reliable witness. Cradled in the Recaro sports seats, Jack enjoyed watching the blue illumination needle climb up the black background of the speedometer. It did confuse him a little as the silver numbers were only calibrated in kilometers. Irish modernization had finally caught hold of the Irish motor codes, they'd gone metric, a few years ago now. But Jack was old school, he still thought in miles. Then he thought who cares what speed I'm doing! Several people looked enviously at him as he passed the Insignia R32 on the grill beaming proudly on behalf of the car's temporary owner.

"Got a car, a 16 Golf, silver with alloys." "Good, good, I'll watch out for you." Before any more conversation could take place, Jack interjected, "Hang on, I'll call you back." He heard the incoming call pips on his phone. Only the shills (coworkers) or the mark [victim] for this sting had this number. When the scam was over the phone would end up in the Shannon River. Timmy had been a shill for him along with some local hired help. He was on the phone to Timmy already and none of the others would have the nerve or reason to ring him. This meant only one thing; the incoming call was from the marks side. As to who and why there was only one way to find out. He checked the screen and saw it was Aidan Cohen's work number. Jack answered the phone by stating his name for the scam alone. "Hello, Richard Wing speaking."

"Hold for Mr. Aidan Cohen," came the monotone and menstrual voice of the secretary. She was followed by some dull panpipe music. Jack tried to contain his annoyance. Didn't anyone realise he was driving? It was illegal to drive and hold anything in Ireland now, let alone a phone. Jack had visions of his whole operation being ruined because of a Garda (just doing his job, of course) pulling him over to ask about the phone currently heating his ear! Wouldn't that Garda be a lucky boyo! A simple traffic violation would net him a lot of fraud case results. As aggravating as this thought train was, it was preventing him from getting a much bigger headache. Why was Aidan Cohen ringing him now and when exactly would he condescend to talk to him?

Having spent time doing the work of the bailiff which started this whole sorry vendetta, Aidan himself noticed the desperation of the punters he affected. And so, he became a loan shark, small time at first. His specialty was bleeding the working classes who just wanted a good Christmas or a new TV. Just because he wore a suit and operated his sharking in the disguise of a legitimate banker, he prospered. From the man on the street who just wanted the simple pleasures Aidan earned huge interest and soon rose up the financial rankings. He started tidying up people's affairs, advising where to reinvest their money. His talents were noticed by some in the criminal fraternity who rewarded him well for his efforts on their behalf. His fortune consequently rose rapidly. Any normal management checks and balances were castrated by Cohen, neutralising the other members of the bank management team with his "sly dig." The campaign described earlier to discredit his rivals. His bank (and it was his alone) might never take on the high street heavies, but he was still worth a few good million. The fifty Jack and the crew were taking would not damage his lifestyle one little bit. Jack, of course, told himself this, to make it easier to do. The truth is this money had taken Cohen a few good years to accrue.

He was corrupt. To work with some of his clients, that was a requirement. So, guilt was not going to be a factor. They weren't exactly taking out of the mouths of orphaned children, or anything like it.

Another thing that made him the perfect mark was, of course, that they had no previous connection. Ireland was a small place and the fact that two criminals hadn't encountered each other was quite rare. This enforced waiting was telling on Jack. He wasn't sure as to what Cohen was capable of! Why ring now?

"Come on. Pick up. You rang me, remember!" Jack shouted at the panpipe noise. He now started to second guess himself. He'd always done small time crime. Had he gone too big this time? Was revenge going to unravel on him? He felt that he had got the balance right. Whatever the problem, that was not it!

Still listening to the panpipes, Jack was ready to burst. Still self-doubt was growing within him as he now in his head went over the scam in every detail. The idea was loosely based on the Nigerian advance fee fraud as mentioned in many papers over the years. The 4-1-9 frauds are so called after the Penal Code in Nigeria that they violate. The con is well flagged around the world. The Gardai even has a five-page article on it on their website. The brilliance this time was that Jack's crew really thought they'd made it believable. Normally it worked as follows.

An individual or company receives a communication from an alleged official representing a foreign government or agency. The person (s) involved are instructed that due to a cockup of huge proportions, (this is phrased slightly differently in the sting mail,) the Nigerian government have a huge amount (anywhere between 10 and 60 million) in dollars untouchable to them. The way the funds could be accessed is through a foreign account. If you agree to help you can keep 25%. All you have to do is furnish your

details, bank identity etc. make a trip to Nigeria to tidy up
loose ends and as easy as that Ireland has yet another multi-
millionaire! Jack remembered when the Irish had nothing.
Now thanks to the property boom people have money. In
many cases more than necessary. Plenty of gullible and
greedy people took up these 4-1-9 offers and felt the sting
later.

Cohen was a lot of things, but gullible was not one of them.
Had they been rumbled? Was that the reason for this call?
The crew knew they were entering dangerous territory.
That's why theirs was so much cleverer a scam than the
straight 4-1-9. They used the idea of a dodgy third world
country with corruption. They gave a free trip to Nigeria to
seal the deal. However, instead of giving free money, they
offered a good return of 50% in one year on Cohen's
investment. First, they made contact electronically and then
in person. They purported to be Irish businessmen with
contacts in the Nigerian government. They explained that
they had developed these contacts to the point that they
were getting offers of huge exclusive contracts in I.T. This
seemed reasonable, as Ireland was fast becoming an I.T.
hub for Europe. Timmy had been able to use his I.T.
background to flesh out the cover story. They identified the

problem that they had to be a lack of venture capital. This they openly admitted was not for software/hardware. Those deals were already done. This money, they specified fifty million, was for backhanders to guarantee the granting of contracts. They explained that it didn't matter where the money came from, as it was illegal to give these backhanders. However, after the year was up on receipt of first profits (150%) would be returned legally, i.e., Cohen could use them to launder dirty cash. If the first deal became good, there would be more deals and a further opportunity to clean cash. To prove this to anybody took a lot of paperwork. That cost! Cohen even got flown to Nigeria with Delaney to meet one of their contacts. All of these deductibles meant that the 50 million would be more like maybe 47½ million by the end of the project. This of course even for Delaney was still a huge haul. But had he made very little out of it, Delaney would still proceed, revenge was a motivator here too. The expenses though were worth it, as they gave the whole scam a believability that Cohen would not see through.

At least Delaney hoped as much. But this call may tell him otherwise. Although the way it was going the R32 would have him there in not too long, so the phone would not be necessary. He could ask in person.

A cyclist pulled out of the bike lane to overtake a fellow peddler right in front of Jack who broke hard and shouted at the cyclist.

Aidan Cohen's voice finally came on the line. Jack thought no more of the one-man peloton, the yellow shirted pedal rotating ape would not spoil the work. The con was on.

SWEETHEART DEALS
1960

Ivan Boswell was a trier. Various ventures in entrepreneurship had failed. Banks were becoming nervous about dealing with him. This latest venture in logistics and storage was under pressure. He needed a prestigious client to come on board and just get this first Bedford truck paid for. Then he stood a chance. He was not above begging. An old girlfriend had been given a senior position with the crowd she now worked for. He resolved to go see her and see if she would help.

Having jumped into the car he remembered how this girl was so big in his life as a teen, how he thought she would be the one. How they grew in what he thought was mutual affection for one another. But out of nowhere she announced she was off to fulfill herself. And like that she was gone, only now to be back but having reached a management position.

He only had a short commute before he found himself heading up the long driveway of the big house. Once arrived at the turning circle at the front door, he then alighted from the car and banged on the self-same front door. Staff came and permitted him entry, then showed him to the drawing room. They said they would let him go in himself.

This he did and sat in front of her. She was busy with some desk chores, shuffling paper. "Hello Dymphna," he said looking at the top of her desk facing head. "It's Mother Superior Dymphna now Ivan," she replied in a schoolteacher to pupil kind of way. Then she let her defenses down. "How have you been?" He couldn't help himself. "You mean since you left me high and dry?"

And so up went the defenses again. She explained what he already knew. As he was a Proddie and she a good Catholic girl it just couldn't have worked. Even if they could figure it out, society wouldn't. They would be pariahs, proper persona non grata, both together and individually. The longer she spoke the more she became nunish, very proper in her demeanor.

Ivan didn't agree with her assessment in truth. His take was that she was a coward to give them up so easily. A beautiful coward. There was now Mrs. Boswell but he still thought often about what might have been. But debating it now was to alienate a potential investor. So he moved the conversation on and told her he needed her help.

"I just need a good regular customer to help me get over the early stages."

As he pleaded, she countered with how the convent itself was struggling in these straightened times. She also made the point that even if she could help, they weren't exactly awash with the kind of work a logistical firm could provide. He pleaded on optimistically, increasing the manipulation factor by leaning across the table and tenderly taking her hand as a lover would, as opposed to an acquaintance. It had been ten years since she fled to the monastical safety of the veil.

He looked at her and reassessed her with the ten years of mileage and had to admit she still looked good for it. He was jerked back into reality by his next thought, that she was assessing him in the same way. She was too. All so quietly unable to prevent a smile of appreciation, subtle though it was from giving her away.

He got out of the seat and went around to her side of the desk. Again, he took her hand and looked deeply into her eyes. Theirs was a passion not so much of the unrequited but unfulfilled kind.

"Dymphs," he whispered as he allowed his forehead to touch hers. At least as much as was uncovered by her coif. Her nunish attire was designed to make intimacy uncomfortable at every level.

Looking back at him, she had a thought. A light bulb moment that explained her quick but nontraditional rise up the ranks. She had done the required ten years of service, but still a few years light of forty and so smashing that particular glass ceiling. Ivan knew of her exquisite intellect and had no bother seeing the merit of being rewarded by her peers. Her quick thinking here just confirmed it for him. "What if there was a way?" "What?" "I'll show you." She rose and by placing her hand in his, guided him to follow. As she got to the door, she released her grip and became penguin like again. Ivan followed her. As he did, he remembered walking across dance hall floors in 1950 with her and dancing cheek to cheek to Mona Lisa by Nat King Cole. It was lovely and romantic and perfect as a breakup song too. So, it came in useful when she ran away with the circus so to speak.

(Obviously if we ever make a film this will have to make the soundtrack. Your choice to @nellieskids1.)

The lover's language is universal and so Cupid slings his arrows far and wide. For instance, Nellie's torch burned bright for Master Murphy. She pined and wished. They flirted but remained unrequited. How could she show courage and ask him out? The emancipation of the free loving 60's hadn't quite arrived. At least not here in BallyGortMore. Brave and bold was still second to prudish conservatism. What an idea! No girl could be that forward. Silly and outrageous.

ITS COMPLICATED

2023

"Sorry to keep you waiting Richard." "That's OK Aidan. I'm almost with you." "Yes good, that's why I'm ringing you. Slight change of plan! I know we arranged to meet at my office. Can't do it you see. I've had some unexpected visitors. The C.A.B. boys, they are tearing my place apart. Although why they are looking at me is a mystery. I'm an honest businessman with nothing to hide."

Delaney a.k.a. Wing swallowed his laugh. C.A.B. or Criminal Assets Bureau has probably had more than one look at Cohen, just as he did. Aidan was quite calm about it and so Delaney surmised that he must run his less legit operations from a separate office unknown to the C.A.B. and him for that matter. "Anyway, we can still meet, somewhere different, that's all." Jack didn't like the change of plans at any stage of a project let alone the final one. Planning was the key to his survival, especially at this level of risk. However, he was a good judge of character and going on Cohen's tone he felt this was all genuine. He was also relieved to be honest at not being rumbled. He was so sure that's what the delay meant. With the natural difficulty that comes from having a phone conversation whilst driving, he awkwardly wiped his brow. Having one hand on the wheel, the phone under his chin and the other hand fumbling for a hanky is one of the many situations frowned on by the Irish traffic corps. For good reason as the Golf did cross lanes involuntarily at the same time.

Regaining control Jack repositioned himself in the left lane approaching the lights and his next left turn. "So where did you have in mind then Aidan?" he asked in much the same tone as if inquiring about the destination of their next Sunday drive.

"A friend owns a student bar in the city centre. Guilds on Denmark St. It does all its biz at the end of the week or on a Wednesday or Thursday night with students. This early on a Monday, it's empty! I know it's not normally where you or I would frequent but I am on a schedule. These C.A.B. guys want me nearby in the event of any discoveries. That place is only 5 minutes away, you understand." Jack understood alright. To make the best money of his life he had to go along with it all. "No sweat, see you there." Jack signed off.

It was now only 10:25am. The traffic was kind to Jack. He was only a block away from the pub rendezvous in one direction and he noted a block from the car park where Timmy should be looking after the bread and butter. Aidan had a few blocks to cross and would probably have to perform an Oscar winner to elude the Asset Bureau people for the half hour. Jack decided that he had time to nip along to the car park and check out how Timmy was getting on. He also decided to drive there, as at least he'd get parking.

The Milk Market car park was an enclosed car park. Enclosed interestingly not by a gawdy fence with a spiky head on it but by a series of terraced shops with timber shutters. All little independent outfits; taking on their financially mammoth competitors with pride. One of them Jack even supported when he was in the area, a quaint cafe/ chipper. He liked their onion rings. The whole place was restored at huge cost sometime back in the 90s and was now also a thriving farmers market. This was a very apt place to do a merchandise deal. Its history demanded that much. There were only two gates into the courtyard, one of which was pedestrianised by half the wrought iron gates being closed and the six resident 1100-litre wheelie bins placed in front of it. The roof covering the terrace of shops also covered the gates area creating an arch effect. At the pedestrian end, this ensured that car park custom and general passers used the gated area as a shelter from the rain. The sudden shower came as Jack drove inside. As he located space and engineered his taking it, he saw Timmy in the Transit. They saluted each other as if surprised to see each other. In Timmy's case this was surprising as he'd not expected to see Jack quite so soon. "How'ya?" Jack inquired. "Grand what are you doing here?" came the reply.

Jack spent the next 5 minutes bringing Mac up to speed on their marks change of plan, concluding with, "So anyway that's where I'll be when you finish here. What's happened with you?" "The lads have taken the first load off me; this is the 2nd." Mac pointed in the back as he continued, "They agreed with me 950 the lot, but they want 200 back for luck. I think I can get them to agree to 100." Jack's brain was on overtime now working out yesterday's take; 850 + 2400 for other stings that's 3250 for one day's work, not bad. Timmy was staring towards the car entrance looking out for the traders. "Fifty million would be better," he said. Jack just smiled and nodded his approval. "Lookout, here they come," Timmy observed.

They pulled into the neighboring space and got out, three big fisted, beer gutted, fast talking traders. They knew Jack as well as Timmy and welcomed him by opening their fists flat and offering the firmest of handshakes. "They are good clothes, this time Jack sir, there's no denying." "Glad you're happy Sheamie boy," Jack replied. "Got to go now, I leave ye with Timmy." With this Jack made for the exit. He had to shuffle his way through the rain shelter whose inhabitants had all now taken to their smokes. As he walked up the street, he took advantage of all the clean shop windows to check his reflection, making the needed adjustments. Had to look his best after all!

Meanwhile Timmy helped the three men to load from his to their Transit. His, a white 06 reg with a few dents, torn seat fabric and a blown bulb or two, contrasted poorly with their freshly washed and polished red 17 reg. All the while he bantered with them defending as much of his luck money as possible. These negotiations haven't changed down the ages. People have always enjoyed the fun of making the deal. Timmy recalled how on a different day one of the traders bragged to all who would listen and how he bought a Toyota Dyna for just €1700 from a local timber merchant. The buying of the Dyna was not what brought the pride.

No, it was the deal breaking, what did that. The trader knew the truck was advertised at €2200 but only offered €1200. The merchant's wife was handling the sale and reminded him of her price. They gradually both gave ground finishing at €1750. The trader rowed away, insisting on a hundred back for luck to finish at €1650 but the owner's wife said no! This went on for a solid half hour till the husband, the merchant himself got the two of them to split the difference bringing the final price to €1700. Deal done!

In fact, the vendors made a good profit on the transaction. They too, as did the traders, enjoyed every minute of the trading. To Timmy, however, it wasn't about having fun but merely making profits. He was also conscious that Jack was expecting his backup on request. It was 10:57am now and today's deal was worth a lot, so now came the time to call it on the value of the clothes. Timmy capsized on the luck money a bit sharpish. He was out of time and still making good money. The traders took their success graciously, suggesting to Timmy a celebration drink and that they were buying! "Sorry lads, another meeting! Us entrepreneurs never stop, you know what I mean..." Timmy carried on thanking them for the offer and suggested maybe next time, and then he got back into his now almost empty van.

Timmy looked at his watch. It was not funny. He would have to hurry up. It was nearly time for today's big operation to get under way. He would be there with ringside seats (earphones at least).

DEAL BREAKING

The traders left through the same exit as Jack, saying they'd just have the one. Timmy made sure they'd all gone before he searched the rear cargo area. He reached in and retrieved a toughened black plastic case. It had big bulky red plastic buckles clipping it shut. This gave it the appearance of a DIY tool carry case. You know the type that get most men excited, because these reinforce the idea that they know what they're doing when knocking that hole in the wall or putting up the shelves. The more of these cases you have, the more confident you'll be! He unsnapped the buckles and revealed a gray foam bed in a case protecting what looked like a Walkman (that's an antique music player from the 1980s). This was what was called in the movies a wire. Or at least this was the signal receiver. Jack had the microphone taped to his chest.

As an aside, Timmy grinned, now recalling Jack being grumpy when fitting it. It was uncomfortable, he had said. It was making his white chest hair itchy, he had said. None of that mattered if it meant that Timmy could hear Jack. He might need to deploy his parachute, his safety word, RUM

& COKE. He would be glad of it then. He turned it on, nothing! "You have got to be kidding me!" he shouted.

The batteries were dead, no red light to show it working so Timmy was out of the van as quick as lightning. He asked for directions to the nearest shop likely to sell batteries. Here he made another mistake because he asked a woman shopper loading her car, who actually wanted to help. This meant that she took her time in answering and asked silly questions like, "Are you walking, or do you have your car?" Eventually he got his answer and ran for it, only two minutes away. They were in the city center after all. Then two minutes back. The whole episode took maybe 8 or 10 minutes. As Timmy was running to and fro, he couldn't help but think briefly then that it really was time that they modernised their equipment. Nowadays these things can be charged and don't need separate batteries.

Hopefully Timmy had not missed anything like Jack being kneecapped or something. On the way over and back he also wondered who had the receiver last. Whoever it was, he or Jack, must have left the receiver switched on, thus running down the batteries. Now safely back in the van, he replaced the duds and switched on and listened.

Jack was now one corner away from the meeting place. It was 11:13am. Cohen and co would surely be inside by now. Jack rounded the corner and grabbed at his case. He opened it whilst balancing it against his chest. Jack was now starting to feel another adrenaline rush as he checked inside for all his props. Satisfied, he put the case to the classic arm's length professional holding position. It was a streamline executive supplied to him by an overzealous Amway salesman, a very long time ago. It suited him, especially when dressed in full business regalia, as he was now. His McGee suit (green with occasional and faint blue fleck) was well tailored and gave him the look of a hungry businessman whilst his oak leaf sheepskin coat (brown obviously) went as far as his thighs and really gave him the look of accomplishment.

He approached the bar. From the outside it looked very American Western. The front was large glass windows all etched with the message "Enjoy Budweiser at Guilds" and were surrounded in a very striking pine/ beeswax effect timber. The only clues that you were not in the American Wild West came when you looked back from a distance. Then you saw the next-door shop accessorised with its rubbish bin outside it. This was knocked over and laid on its side by a wino down and out type sitting with his legs outstretched in the service entrance to the left of the pub. The bin was being repurposed as a wind breaker by him. On the footpath were a few items of rubbish blowing slowly by the pub. These were not from the bin as you might expect. This was as a result of littering. This modern and yet universal problem is hard to imagine outside the Alamo.

"Take a deep breath Jacko," Jack said to himself. As he reached for the bar door, he thought it'll all be over soon. He immediately appreciated being inside as the weather, although not raining right now, was blowing at a bit of a gust. The rain threatened a return. The weather's effect was softened on entering the bar. Instead, Jack felt a huge swirl of hot air blowing from the air conditioner over the door. Considering the power it was using, the unit was remarkably quiet and so Jack had no problem hearing Aidan Cohen welcome him to the pub. Neither did Timmy who was listening from 5 minutes away.

"Good morning, Mr. Wing. You found it alright, did you?" opened Cohen. Jack responded with, "yes, no bother." He was phony in his enthusiasm. He wanted to sweeten Cohen in as many discreet ways as possible. You could call it a form of deal breaking. "Your directions were right on the money." He knew that once Cohan took control of the repartee, he'd also have the deal. Jack didn't want that, of course, so how to keep sweetening the mark without being too obvious, that was the problem.

He moved deeper into the bar over to Aidan Cohen's table. In crossing the room, he inhaled the smells abundant, stale beer, the occasional wisp from the smoker's area of foulness, the putrid stench from the toilets. This was a proper den of iniquity. Jack's solution on how to keep Cohen sweet was a gamble. Fitting, given the setting.

"You often have visits from the authorities or are you just now getting their attention?" Cohen paused before answering, giving an edge to the conversation that Jack couldn't read through. He hoped that by drawing attention to the C.A.B. visits today, Cohen would receive it as a compliment. It was something to brag about amongst criminals, not being caught but getting attention. Ego would encourage him to seek it. To Jack, forgetting anonymity with the authorities was sloppy from the criminal tradecraft point of view. But crooks like Cohen had a large ego. Hopefully, he'd want to revel in it and Jack desired him to. So did young Timmy. (To Jack, Timmy was like a younger brother, hence he regarded him as "young Timmy," but the gap of only a few weeks ensured Timmy believed the boss did not have the advantage on him age wise.) He may have been a short walk away but there and then he was in that pub, behind Jack understanding his tactic and praying for success.

"Ah yes, sorry about all this, frightful bore I know, nature of the thing, you know. Everybody wants my money. I decide who I'm going to give it to though."

"Exactly right. We work hard for it, we earn it. We should be the ones who reinvest it too. I couldn't agree more." Now down to business he thought as he carried on.

"You've had a good look at our proposal and what do you say sir?"

Cohen rebuffed "You don't do small talk do you, Wing? Where is your sidekick? Are we not waiting for him?"

"My sidekick, I…. yes, you mean young David. (Timmy was covered as David Trent.) He will not be joining us today. He's looking after another deal for me as we kind of got ourselves double booked today. Before I go any further though I must apologise for that. I know David is my I.T. specialist, it would have been good to have him here to handle any last-minute questions. But as you know we must send the funds to guarantee people over there will cooperate. David can answer any I.T. queries from you, any other day. To reassure you I've brought copies of all the supporting papers, the figures, and the written but unofficial promises from these people. Most of all I bring you and remember that it is I saying this …. I've had many deals with them, the Nigerians. I bring you a chance to make things even harder for C.A.B. to find. These people will be laundering your money back as long as we can keep buying their attention. What do you think?"

Cohen did not answer. Just sat quietly, although Timmy heard people breathing as he was biting the steering wheel in the van.

Jack had played the situation as well as he could. The wire feed went very quiet. The silence was deafening, the tension escalating.

Cohen did eventually oblige with a further inquiry. "You mean there might be more opportunities?" Greed was wonderful that way. He stalled a bit as if he still had no decision made. "The C.A.B. thing is just a formality. They'll not find anything." He didn't care what Richard Wing thought of him. He just needed a second or two to think.

"I'm in. Deal done." Jack acknowledged that was excellent. He of course was relieved but couldn't show it. Instead, he kept up a sober front. Timmy on the other hand did not. The van was jiggling under the duress of Timmy's celebrations. He was in public view. At least two or three look towards the man. He didn't have to keep it in; his public wouldn't overreact to his punching the air. Jack's audience would be asking funny questions if Jack did as Timmy did. Timmy was still in the van screaming yes, yes, yes. Jack was signing papers and taking delivery of the tablet. Cohen explained that the Bitcoin wallet and the word file containing the passwords were all on the tablet.

Next came the sit-down meal where Jack small talked with Aidan for a while. Jack entertained by showing some of his true self talking of an exhibition match between Ken Doherty and Jimmy White that was due in Tipperary town the following week. Of course, that meant he couldn't possibly go as he might meet a very sore Cohen there trying for him and the 50 million. Jack didn't think that far ahead, he was just glad to speak of one of his passions for a change. It also distracted Jack from his nerves, he'd almost pulled it off. The tablet he had unlocked a lot of money to him. All he had to do now was get it safely to Timmy and then dreams would come true.

Timmy had got over his excitement and was now in a Zen-like prayer mode. He was eager for Jack's safe exit and return to the van. Jack also was now noticing that Cohen was not alone. He had an escort, a big guy who could do a lot of damage to Jack's physique given the chance. Please God it wouldn't come to that. They moved on to drinks. Jack used the driving laws as an excuse to stop at the one pint. He was then going to make his exit. Looking out at the spitting which had started since he entered the pub but then had got heavier, he spoke of the lovely Limerick weather. It takes huge stupidity to believe that it rains more in

Limerick than anywhere else. It's not Angela's Ashes, he thought. Putting on his herd of sheep, he was now door bound. It was all going really well. If it had been a Hollywood flick or even a Pinewood Love Actually effort, the soundtrack for right now would be something of a feel-good vibe. The whole cinema would sing along with Jack. "Ah yes, I'm the great pretender."

(Another good choice here, The Man Who Faked His Own Life by Eleanor McEvoy. Just curious, what feel good songs would you include? I'd love to know, post me @nellieskids1. Who knows if there is ever going to be a movie soundtrack or indeed a movie? I can dream!)

But now you know how it is: music players are notorious for letting you down at the critical moment. CDs stick, records jump. Even the popular music streamers are only as good as the internet they are streamed on.

LUSTFUL EYES
1962

"Horses'" cloth flat cap bounced on the dashboard of the jeep, as the terrain interrupted the smoothness of the ride. "Thanks so much, Mr. Flanagan. I didn't fancy getting wet there." "Shur, wasn't I heading this way anyhow," he replied.

Obviously, he needed to keep a look at the road. But he had a good-looking girl now in close range. Who wouldn't sneak a look? She had a fine pair of boots on, dirty as they were. A polish would be welcome, missy. Bright white socks just above the boots and then lovely white calves swallowed up by a half-length green skirt. It had some pattern upon it, and he couldn't make it out. He couldn't ogle. And yet he noticed her top was covered in the same pattern. He observed it as best he could, the movement of the terrain as it translated into chest movements of that pattern.

"Thanks again," she said seeing her gate approaching. "We've a nice few horses in the yard if you ever fancy a look. Call in, why don't you?" he said back to her. She closed the door behind her and headed inside. He looked at her for a second. A quick fiddle of gears and he was moving again.

He was thinking how had he not noticed her before? Perhaps, it was her coming of age lately. Was she 17 or 18, he wasn't sure? She was young, true enough but still womanly, almost alluringly so. The beguiler! He drove his way home with a big smile across his face. It mattered not to him but as a point of accuracy, the reader should note Miss Nellie was in fact all woman, being 21years of age.

MOMENTS OF TRUTH
2023

Jack really did feel it was going all his way. He was on cloud nine as he reached the door. With one hand on the brass door handle, he turned and smiled at the suckers. He was just saying his final goodbyes when that CD did indeed skip. If this was that Hollywood production, as mentioned previously, this would be where they play the high pitch screech to indicate a scratch on the record. From outside in the rain, came in three very happy men. As Jack saw them in his peripheral vision, he bowed his head low, hoping they would not acknowledge him. It was too much to ask for on this occasion, for they gave Jack a terrific salute. "We'll have to do more business, Jacko. A good day's work, eh?" Jack was out the door before they had completed the pronouncement. He tried once out of the pub to upgrade his movement from fast walk to canter to full on gallop.

Cohen barked at his hired hand, "Don't let him out of your sight, until I know what's going on. Bring him back here if you can catch him." Andrew Finley was the help's name.

He was Cohen's driver, fixer and bodyguard. He was from Australia originally and qualified as a tiler. He came to Ireland in the very early 90s when the current boom had yet to bed down. There was not enough work to stay in his trade. In looking for an alternative he observed that he was quite a fit man. Years on a good diet, Australian sun, in a physical job had seen to that. He had to use that to his advantage. He got the position of bouncer for the local nightclub or disco's as they were still called back then. He was good at his job.

As Cohen was rising in stature, evolving from loan shark to bank manager to bank owner, he recruited protection from the personal security industry. He soon hired Finley who was now head of Cohen's security team. As the boom grew he often toyed with the idea of giving up and going back to his trade. The work would be there now in bucket loads was his thinking. Finley, however, had grown used to basking in the reflected glory of Cohen. Even though it was involuntary he liked the respect people gave him due to his association with Cohen. He signaled to one of the lesser henchmen to comply with Cohen's orders. As the guy who incidentally had the same physique as Finley but a lot less brain cells, went out the door, Cohen said to the three strangers, "So I gather you've done good business today. Why don't I buy you all a drink and you can tell us about it?"

"Mr., we don't want no drink from you, our business is our business!" one of the traders replied. All three turned their backs to Cohen and company and were deciding what to drink, discussing what could have spooked Delaney when they heard the click of a handgun being readied for firing. The few innocent bystanders who were sitting in the bar mid meal suddenly jumped up, made their excuses and left. Cohen didn't seem to even notice them. He, having the stage presence of a lead actor, had the three boys' full attention.

"Gentlemen I don't want any trouble. Tell Desiree, that lovely barmaid there, what you want to drink. I'll buy and then come and sit with me. I've just a few questions for you. There may even be money in it for you."

"Just one drink. You did ask nicely, I guess one won't hurt, eh boys?" said the smallest of them. The other two quickly agreed. All three ordered a Guinness from Desiree who looked very frightened by the entire goings on. She was quite a strong woman but guns being waved around today would make anyone's lips quiver. She knew more of Cohen than today. She had seen him reprimand other business acquaintances. When getting stock from the stockroom to the right of the pub once, she found the employee of Cohen's unconscious from a beating he had got for dishonesty. He had skimmed from one of Cohen's deals. Only someone stupid would stand up to Cohen and stupid she was not. She'd keep her head down and serve the drinks.

By the time the stouts were settled the three traders had joined Cohen at his table. Desiree brought them over, dutifully served them and returned behind the counter without a word. She then relied on an old trick of the bar trade. She picked up a cloth and pretended to clean. She was listening to everything she could hear from the Cohen party although they were now in a deliberate struggle to remain discreet. A virtual whisper was all she could hear.

Again, she swiped her finger along her scar line. She had it a time now, it itched at her, in anxious times. She could rely on her irritant; in the same way an arthritic person knew rain was due as a result of a flare up. She itched and so she knew it was not going to be a good day.

"OK guys, the man who left here just now has taken something belonging to me. I want it back," Cohen opened, holding his hand to his chest to signify the return to him of what was his.

"What's that to us?" they had the small one reply. He was now their duly elected leader.

"Nothing," returned Cohen, abruptly cutting him off. "For now, I ask the questions, or Finley here will have to talk on my behalf, if you know what I mean." He pointed at the gun bulge. "OK, you called him Jacko. What's his full name?"

The lads felt most decidedly as though they were turning into what everybody hates. Use the colloquialisms of squealer, rat, fink, tout or even a telltale tattler, nobody likes an informer. Even parents who love their children as only they can, soon tire of a telltale child. However, to be a hero now would certainly not benefit them. The sight of the handgun in Finlay's underarm area eliminated any small agony gone through in making the decision to cooperate. It was clearly visible as a bulge in the shape of Finley's suit jacket. The three men didn't identify the gun because like Delaney, they knew nothing about them. Had they'd been able to recognise it, they would have known it as a Beretta 9000 pistol - small, compact and heavier than you might think. It is a self-loading pistol, chambered for 9mm parabellum rounds and designed to be a lethal firearm. Most bodyguards that Finlay knew carried this weapon on account of the fact that it was specifically designed for self-defence. A most welcome feature that Finlay relied on, was the finger rest that could be adjusted – lowered for those with large hands or raised for those whose hands were smaller. Finlay's finger rest was always in the lowered position, to accommodate his beefy digits.

If they knew how much damage it could do, then they would probably have cried or fainted. Instead, they simply answered the question. "Jack Delaney, he's a well-known con to those that need to know. He comes from somewhere in Tipperary. Not sure where!"

Cohen looked steamed as the reality of things was settling. "A tall whiskey, Desiree." "What about his partner?" was Cohen's next question.

"Timmy McGuire, sir, from Tipp too, sir. They've been together a fair while," the traders answered in chorus now. They explained that was all they knew and asked to be excused. They asked in much the same tone as when the children asked their teachers could they go to the loo. Instead of "An bhfuil cead agam dul amach go dtí an leithreas?" they said, "We told you what you wanted, can we go now so?" Aidan Cohen said no. They try it again this time standing up to leave. Finley took out the weapon he had concealed and waved it, at first at them, then at their still warm seats. The message was sit down or be shot. No words needed. Nothing like a game of charades to help take your mind off your worries. Cohen asked his next question.

"So, on this job in Nigeria, you know anything?" They all said nothing. One even volunteering that cons don't advertise or brag about their scams. That only happens in the movies. The final contribution from the traders was that likely there was no deal in Nigeria. He'd been set up. Cohen normally was really very restrained. He'd often de-stressed by popping the odd pill or taking a snort of something. These were not to hand, and he was angry. Veins started to rise up in his neck and face. He grabbed the table using his normally yellow stained fingers. His grip was so tight that a nivea complexion deleted the smoke stains from his hands momentarily. He flung the table so hard that it landed on its side, in front of the bar counter hatch door, like a barricade. Its chipped legs pointing out towards the bar, revealing the underbelly of the table. Multicolor fragments of gum clung on as if to say, "Didn't get us off the table, did you tough guy?" Seeing the situation unfolding Desiree was so glad to have the barricade.

She channeled all her trust into that piece of wood. She continued to load the dishwasher. She would clean up when Cohen had gone, either that or if he told her to do so. There was no way she'd climb the barricade until then. Beyond this, was now officially no [wo] man's land. The noise of all the glass (and there was a lot of it given this was the second time Cohen had drinks with people today) was as if a car had smashed through the main front window in the bar. It was everywhere, all over the floor, on the upholstery and even had bounced off the floor on impact and landed on some of the vending machines between the bar and the toilets. Some of it was clear, some opaque, some green, and some brown. So many different shapes. There were large and small fragments, each piece is unique as a snowflake. They seemed as numerous as sand grains. And in the same way as those sand grains annoy beach picnickers by turning up inside both their sandwiches and socks, glass shards would be found still clinging to hiding places in the upholstery and filling little fissures in the floorboarding for ages yet.

Had Jack actually been there and allowed himself the pleasure of finding a funny side to it all, he might have allowed his raconteur persona to surface and told his story. A true story of one of the first scams he had ever learned. It was on school holidays around the time of the teacher-student bookie incident. You could say it was at the more innocent stage of his career path.

It involved glass, making it topical to this scene. A good conversationalist always knew when to be topical. He would have regaled them all with the tale of his job with the fair. He charged fifty pence, old Irish, for one go at his attraction. He stood two bottles up at the end of a wooden bowling alley of about three or four feet and just one foot wide. The idea was a prize was won if you knock both down (breaking them not necessary.) Jack would enjoy explaining how he could attract his custom. "Come on sir. Have a go, win a prize for herself, sir. It's only fifty pence and all I need you to do is knock over the bottles... you will, sir. Excellent. Take out your silver then, sir. One coin, one go. OK. You roll the ball, sir. If your hand crosses the start line, it's disallowed. If you roll too hard and the ball hits the back wall, it's disallowed. It's easy, sir. Good luck sir." Then Jack would have enjoyed explaining how after three or four goes that the punter would give up. To finish and really impress the group Jack would finally explain to them, who would be trying desperately not to crunch anymore glass into the solid oak floorboards, how he took so much money off the gullible fools. Perhaps the bar girl might suggest the bottles were glued down. He'd say no, but in case the punters thought that, during the sting he'd lift them (the bottles not the punters) up to show them that they were not. At last, by way of climax, he'd explain that if two bottles were put beside one another with one slightly forward creating a diagonal line if looked down from above and about 5 millimeters between the two then a fall of both was literally impossible. Money for jam.

(Quirky soundtrack song choice here, I've Got A Lovely Bunch Of Coconuts.)

However, Jack was not here now. As much as his returning would cheer up Cohen, it was not likely to occur.

Cohen took his smartphone from his pocket. Like all phones today, it could do a lot more if only Cohen understood it. He was more a "phones are for calling people, kind of guy." Delaney and he had that much in common at least. That is along with the fifty million other reasons, they now shared. He accessed his dialed numbers menu and hovered over Wing's a.k.a. Delaney's number. He pressed the green button and as he waited for the call pickup, he felt very similar to how Jack had felt earlier, when he had been kept waiting on the phone.

Jack at that moment was involved in a bit of a high-speed chase across the city. Timmy was at the wheel of the R32. Jack had run to the junction at the roads end, to meet Timmy who had swapped the van for the car. The lesser goon was now in hot pursuit. His Beemer was perhaps 300 feet behind. On seeing Jack get into the car, he got straight into his. No foot chase meant this was not the most comfortable of leads, especially as a high-speed chase in Limerick city center is actually an oxymoron. The fastest they were traveling, right now, as they got on to Mulgrave

Street was between five and ten miles an hour. The phone
went off alright, but was ignored by Jack, who now wished
he was near the Shannon so he could chuck the phone.
Looking at it, he saw the origin of the incoming call. Cohen
wanted to congratulate him on a good day's work. How
sporting! "Come on, Tim. Can't we go faster?" Jack was
leaning forward willing the speed injection.

"Yeah, of course, right into the back of yer man!" Timmy
was a little frayed but so was Jack who replied, "All right,
all right! We got to think of something. The way we're
going, if he was to have walked, he'd catch us!" In truth,
the stress of the situation was now showing on the pair who
never actually envisaged the way things were turning out.

From the minute Jack got into the car they bickered. Jack's
first words were, "This is all your bloody fault. You had to
meet those eejits today, didn't you?" his rage carried on
another minute or two. Timmy wisely quiet, waiting for a
very agitated Jack to need to catch a breath. When Jack did
pause to inhale, Timmy then cut him off with, "What you
mean my fault? My meet went well, and I heard your deal
on the wire and I'm here for you to pick you up, to save you
from them." Jack spat back, "What do you mean, what do

you mean? I'll tell you what I mean, those three galoots came into that pub like three peacocks. 'Good deal today,' Jacko they said. And that's another thing, they were so happy, they must have robbed you. Fine day, this has turned out to be, I'll tell you."

Timmy admitted finally that he should have made sure they stayed away from the sting. Who cares about the clothes deal now? Surely, they had bigger worries. Anyway, he had 50 million in his case. "Have a break, dopey! We're rumbled," said Jack with a tear in his eye.

"Ah, no," said Jack feeling genuinely nauseous. A stress reflex perhaps, but vomit he did, right between his legs in to the R32 footwell.

"Timmy, we got to go faster, or he'll catch us," he said wiping the sick away from his lips with his hankie. Timmy said he was in the same traffic jam. To catch them he'd have to get out of his car. Timmy turned out to be a prophet. Jack turned to look around having not liked what he last saw in his mirror. "Happy now. Come on," he shouted as he jumped out of the car swinging his executive case. Timmy looked back. The goon had left the Beemer and was gaining ground. "Beautiful," Timmy managed to say as he ran from the R32. They did well as Ricardo seats are molded and not designed necessarily for people making quick exits. Timmy in truth was glad to leave Jack's projectile insides behind. The smell was highly unpleasant.

First Jack in sheepskin running with case, then Timmy in combats behind him. A fair but not inconsiderable distance behind was a big but fit bouncer. As the shops passed by in a blur, people shouted obscenities at the chase. People are like that; push them off the path or splash puddles at them as you run, they will shout at you! The boys were not hanging about to listen to the abuse. They just ran!

A bus was just pulling in at the stop ahead. It was one of those with the concertina middle. Jack scarcely had enough breath left but succeeded in suggesting they get on. Timmy thought madness! They had just abandoned a souped-up car, because of traffic. He said nothing as he was getting tired of running anyway. They got on and pushed their way down the bus. They overpaid as they had no change and were in a hurry. The goon saw this and ran hard, just making the bus before the driver closed the doors. He paid, again giving too much, then took a step onto the bus, looking for his targets. His face turned sour as he saw them. The driver had closed the doors and started to pull out. They were on the footpath outside. When they saw Brutus was getting onboard, they jumped off, using the back door. They smiled at him as they waved him off. He was not amused. He couldn't get to the doors, as people had him corralled in. If he pushed, the gardai would be called. To make it worse the next stop was a good half mile up the road. Jack and Timmy had time to disappear. For Brutus Goon, it was time to phone home.

The blissfully unaware bus driver had the radio on. A traffic announcement alert interrupted the music. ("Limerick city center is gridlocked. We are getting reports of an abandoned car. Left empty by 2 men reports say.")

Finley made the call whispering into Cohen's ear via the two phone handsets. "Damn them!" said Cohen loudly as he swept any remaining intact glass off the counter. "Right, you three." He was looking at the three traders at the time. "I want you to find him for me and bring him to me. €10,000 for each of you when you do." Bored now with the company, he brushed them away. They left the pub dazed by the last fifteen minutes or so. Unsure how it had all happened but nonetheless they were now on a good earner. They were spending the money, mentally all the way back to their van. These guys were used to good earners. It might be from the outcome of a sulkie race or a good old fashioned boxing fight. It often involved a gamble, flutter, or punt, but this opportunity was simpler than all of that. All they had to do was find and shaft Delaney and McGuire. They were two nice guys but that's business.

Meanwhile Cohen dialed the office, not his official one but the unofficial one that Delaney had suspected he had. "Hello JP. My deal today went a little sour. How can I stop the money transfer?" Cohen took on a face of concentration as his assistant reminded him the money was paid over via a Bitcoin transaction. Bitcoin was trying hard to become a new form of currency. It was stored in digital wallets that were password protected. Lose the password lose the access to the Bitcoin therefore lose its value. Lose the device that the wallet is stored on and not be able to key in the password you still lose its value. So, Delaney looked like he was on a winner. He had to be stopped. The tablet had to be got back. Cohen gestured to Desiree to serve him a whiskey. "Where is my whiskey? I called for it ..like three minutes ago." She knew it had to be a Jameson; and it had to be now, or she might find herself out in the cold room.

The traders were Hennessy, Callanan and Hennessy junior (the son of number one). The smallest one, Hennessy, who acted as spokesman earlier, had thick brown straight hair, as did junior who at 5:11 was at least 4 inches taller than his dad. Callanan had curly black locks of hair, growing slightly towards his shoulders. In the rain, due to their good hair coverage, all three felt a bit like human mops. One had a leather jacket on. It was cracking from wear at places. The other two were in German army parkas. When they arrived back to their van, still in the car park, the first thing they noticed was that Timmy's van was still there also. They took down the registration number. Cohen had given them a phone number to contact him when they had news. He wouldn't expect to hear from them so soon. They would earn their money really easy. "Hello Mr. Cohen, sir. We have news. We found their van from this morning." said spokesman Hennessy.

"You sure it's his?" Cohen inquired.

"It must be," came back the answer. They always used this van on previous deals. Cohen encouraged, responded by asking for the registration. He took note of it as it was called out to him - 96 T etc., etc. He thanked them and suggested that they blend in and wait around awhile for fear that they come back. He'd make contact soon with an address. Perhaps on the other hand he'd send the Aussie. Professional muscle might end this quicker and if it hurt Delaney or Wing or whatever his name is, then so be it. Cohen would ask a guardian of the peace that he could rely on, to run the plate and get the necessary address. This would be cleaned up quickly.

HIDE & SEEK

Jack and Timmy decided to get off the streets. It was a good idea. They ended up in a juice bar painted green with yellow lettering. Sitting in their booth, surrounded by wall-to-wall glass windows. These were the only things separating them from the madness outside, but they still felt safer none the less. It was as if the glass was in fact opaque, they felt less visible. Neither Timmy nor Jack were well informed as smoothie drinkers. Timmy ordered the fruit extreme. This was boastful as it had every fruit available to the bar. If in doubt, try them all (in one glass!). All the running had made both men perspire. Jack took off the sheepskin and draped it over the briefcase that he had already rested on the far side of his seat. He would try a fruit infused iced tea to cool him down. Having vomited earlier he was in no mood for something more exotic.

Timmy took out the tablet and switched it on. A teenager with bad acne brought over the beverages. Timmy connected the tablet to the cafe Wi-Fi. He intended to use the internet to buy something with the Bitcoin. He could start the process to convert the Bitcoin into a genuine currency, spendable how they wanted.

Doing this of course would incur a cost which would erase some of the 50 million. But it meant that they would have the balance to spend how they saw fit. Even if Cohen was to re-acquire the tablet, he would find the Bitcoin wallet empty. The money would be out of his reach.

Jack had some spare time when this was ongoing, so he took hold of the tall glass in which his multicolored cocktail of fruit was contained. He grabbed hold of it in the same way that a peaked capped Irish farmer might have grabbed a pint of stout. Propping his elbows on the table in front of him, his stronger right hand and a vice grip around 70 to 80% of the glass. Raising his right hand to his mouth, he then took what only could be described as a good gulp at it. One full third of the muck was inside him before he recoiled, coughed, and sputtered. In the pandemonium of it all, Jack stood up ensuring another full third ended up on the floor and all over the table. "What is in this? Vile, whatever it is!" Jack shared with the whole of the premises. His face looked as though he still had a mouthful of prunes on board. The juice bar patrons were now looking at Jack.

To them he was the ultimate novice healthy drinker. They enjoyed watching him splutter everywhere, in the same way, the school rebels enjoyed watching a first timer smoke or cough his puff on a cigarette. Timmy, with everyone else, paused to look at Jack.

"Sit down, I have news." Jack obeyed as if he was an employee and not the boss. He took out a hanky and wiped away his newly acquired fruity mustache.

"Did we do it Mac?" Jack asked, eyebrows raised quizzically. Considering the gravity of the news Timmy replied in a very downbeat way. "Yes, I have converted the Bitcoin." He started to sound more excited as he said, "It's now real money, our real money!"

"Yes Jack. We did it!!" The two reached out to each other and jumped and screamed. Both now standing up and jigging together in a kind of, sort of, Irish dance. Again, the whole juice bar suspended their lives to perv on Jack and Timmy. It's not every day that you witnessed two grown men behave as two children.

The lads sat down again and discussed their situation. Timmy reminded Jack of how the money was parceled or divided into fractional packets and was now at their command going from account to account to ensure that no one could track the money to them and their true pick-up place. All they had to do was go there, collect the money and disappear. After a brief but complete daydream on what they would do with their respective cuts, they decided to assess what their next move would be. It was a bit dangerous hanging about here in Limerick as Cohen would be looking for them. Thanks to the traders they were no longer anonymous and so eventually they'd be found. They believed they could risk a short return home to tidy up things before the guards or Cohen got there. They did include the guards as a possibility. Not because of the Cohen sting, he'd say nothing to them. It was because of the abandoned golf. CCTV would be looked at and might give away their identity.

Meanwhile Cohen was playing it cool. He'd been asked back into his office by the C.A.B. boys and girls for another interview. Inside he was raging. At the pub Desiree was still cleaning up the mess of glass and drinks on the floor.

As soon as he could get away from that meeting, he stepped out, took out his phone and pressed redial on Wing a.k.a. Delaney's phone number. By that time Jack and Timmy had agreed that the van had to be moved, if locked in a closed-up car park it might arouse the interest of the authorities, although neither one of them had a good feeling about picking it up, as it was parked so near the pub! Jack knew who was calling. It must be Cohen. Jack imagined that he would have heard the news by now and was very glad a phone was the only connection between the two men right now. Cohen's hands were always clean, precisely because his goons got theirs dirty on his behalf. Jack quivered at the thought of what might happen even yet, if they ever got hold of him and Tim. He had no way of predicting that he, for the most unexpected of reasons, would be talking to Cohen only an hour or so from now. As things stood a chat with Cohen was the last thing he wanted. Ignoring the incoming call ringtone was becoming too much, so it was Timmy who reached for the phone and jabbed at the red cancel button. "How about a cuppa, to refresh our palates after that muck? he asked Jack, who jumped up to get them. Meanwhile Cohen was leaving colourful threats on an answering service that no one would ever listen to!

Timmy grabbed an abandoned red top left across the nearest empty table and started studying the form. On returning with the tea, Jack was not happy to see Timmy tickling his vice. "Don't be at that now, you hear!" Jack announced in exasperation.

"Will we go so?" Timmy asked his shaking coworker. "Yeah, we'd better! Around here is getting kinda claustrophobic," came back Jack. He got up and put the coat back on. The pair, on leaving, made their way back in the direction of the Milk Market. They were both quite cautious, as their route was bringing both uncomfortably close to Aidan Cohen, the pub, the goons, and the guns. If they had borrowed it, they would have left the van there, no question! As it was theirs, it identified them, it had to be moved.

The weather again was closing in and so both buttoned up their jackets to the last. They said nothing, absolutely nothing, to one another all the way back. On arrival back at the car park, both hovered in the archway by the wheelie bins. Several other people had gathered also. They all took to smoking as the rain shower passed off. Pleasantries regarding the weather and the Munster rugby team flew from all directions. Both Timmy and Jack acted as fully involved participants in the discussions. However, what they were really interested in doing was having a look around. No sense in entering the car park if any unwanted attention was within. The walls would make giving any of the same the slip, a good deal trickier. Timmy observed to Jack that the coast seemed clear. No one known to them was visible and the traders van had even been moved. They must have been as eager as he and Jack were to get some distance between the surely raging Cohen. Perceiving it to be safe, both men proceeded into the now sunnier courtyard. The only evidence of the rain as the pair advanced their getaway, was the wet looking concrete on the well surfaced ground. As they got back to the van, a man called from an office window over the main gate. It was the caretaker's office. The man wearing the high visibility jacket was in no way aware of the stress he was causing the two men in calling them. "What does he want?" Timmy grumbled. From Jack came a little reassurance (although he too was nervous.) "It is the caretaker; he probably wants to charge us for the extra time we were here." Jack suggested that he would sort it out whilst Timmy started the engine and began the exit manoeuvre. Timmy agreed, urging Jack to hurry back. He then started an argument that all the older vehicle owners have with their transport, when starting from cold. He exclaimed a chorus of "come on, come on!" as he slowly ground the ignition switch with the key. It replied by making unreassuringly rude noises, suggesting it one day was going on strike if it didn't receive some loving attention soon. After the protest was made, the engine eventually coughed to life. As Timmy was reversing out of the space, he saw that Jack was handing over cash to the attendant. Jack was obviously right about the parking charges. Mid manoeuvre Jack was invisible to Tim due to the blind spot of the van. It was during that time that Jack finished with the car park guy. But it was on walking back to the van, which was now moving, that Jack was called from behind again.

A (DIS) GRACEFUL EXIT

It was the bold Sheamie and his fellow traders. As they came into the car park they called over to Jack. They made a tactical error in declaring Mr. Cohen wanted to chat with him. He knew they had been recruited, so he needed to scarper. So, he ran towards the van. Meanwhile, Timmy had reversed the van. He had opened the side door anticipating the need for a quick escape. He was now driving toward Jack.

Jack, whose adrenaline levels had risen high, was running now full pelt for the van. He had never played rugby. His school was more of a hurling centre of excellence. As an aside he never played much of that either. Therefore, his breath was in rather short supply with all the running. He rather resembles a rugby player though, in that, he was really focused on the task at hand, that of reaching the safety of the van. He subconsciously had decided to throw himself at the van like a rugby player coming in to land a touchdown. (Yes, a try would be more correct here) but a) he didn't know the sport and wasn't up on the terminologies and b) he was a bit preoccupied running for his life, to care.

The entire scene was in flux. The van was now moving towards him. He was in the air now moving towards it when enter stage right, an innocent party. A mother out doing her shopping. Her cocooned baby in front of her acting at this late juncture, as a crutch for the flagging Tamsin. Jack saw her now but was powerless to avoid her. His shoulder jostled her into the van with him. The buggy fell in the melee on its side. The baby was so small his hands were tucked in under a blanket that he was using to keep warm. His harness functioned well, keeping him safe from the fall, although gravity surprised his soother. The poor boy understandably had a good cry as he lay sideways on the ground or rather the buggy did. The doody was now so well out of his reach it may as well have been the whole car park away. The traders, Hennessy Snr and Jnr were the first to circle the child. Callanan was that bit slower to the scene as his focus was initially on the moving van. He only surveyed the scene and became aware of baby having resigned from trying to stop the escaping van. It was getting away. It would not be stopped. The trader's instinct to release the tension would normally involve perhaps waving fists at the van now exiting the car park. A swear word or two would also be normal in these circumstances. But they were now custodians of an innocent. Any passerby would testify, if ever called on, to their frustration. That was still obvious in its manifestation, but it was certainly at the same time, a more muted affair than usual. Let's just say the baby seemed to be having a positive effect.

His mother, now captive, was having an explosion of her senses. What was happening and why could she smell vomit?

SEX ED
1962

Nellie had heard from her father that "Horse" Flanagan was on the way to big things. A man called Tim Vigors had an ambition to go studding globally. He thought Saudi Arabian princes would pay fortunes for good Irish bloodstock. "Horse" meant to beat Vigors to Valhalla. His training form was good. And the covering fees were rolling in. He had been lucky with stallion purchases. Instead of turkeys, he'd got proper athletes. He was wooing the players in Ireland for backing. BallyGortMore will lead the world. Power to him.

It was a Friday morn and Nellie was not due into that shop today until the afternoon. Perhaps she could go up to the stud for a nose about. She was curious as to what went on there and she had an invitation after all. Some tea and toast and off with her.

The day was pleasant and so she soaked up nature, enroute. The birdsong, the bees humming, the breeze swaying the long grasses, gently to-ing and fro-ing. She felt privileged to be here.

As she was reaching the yard, it was a very busy place. A big old lorry had arrived, and its back ramp was dropped. A mare was guided out from within and allowed on a long guide rein to walk off some travel nerves. She was given a drink, access to some food and a rear washdown. She was generally made feel welcome in the yard.

Nell just leaned against a near stable wall and watched. The felt boots were fitted to her hinds. Men tied the mares back legs to prevent any backwards rejection on her part. They wrapped up her tail too to keep it out of the way. "Horse" then signaled for Archibald to be walked in. Another two yard-hands were responsible for that; Johnny Murphy was one of them. He moved as gracefully as the animal he led, in his nearly worn-out wax coat and a short straw hanging from his lower lip. His fringe moving with his every step taken in his Chelsea boots, as was Archibald's mane in rhythm with his front legs. It was poetry: synchronised swimming without any water! She was smitten. She wanted to swoon but just remained motionless, only allowing her eyes to move. Hopefully no one would see the eejit she was being.

No one did because the show was only beginning. All eyes were front and center for the mane event. (Yes, that should be the main event. Just couldn't resist the bad dad pun again. I do love them.) Everyone ready!

The sire was brought to the recipient's rear which he sniffed a bit. Nellie watched nervously as it was her first time seeing this behaviour. On her own farm, they fed and fattened up some sheep and cattle and sold them on. She was naïve about any form of reproduction, animal or otherwise. Something was wrong so they allowed the stallion some slack to guide him around to face the mare.

Nellie imagined they were saying hello and maybe getting to know one another as you do. After a minute or so they went back to the original position. Nellie saw, as everyone else did, what followed. Archibald bit the mare's mane. And then it was over. Nellie noticed the sunlight rippling on the stallion's back leg. Then she giggled as she realised how the shape of the hind leg reminded her of a chicken drumstick from a Sunday dinner. Round and fleshy on top, skinny and bony on the bottom.

The lorry took back its borrowed mare. She was happy to be back to the familiar and gave the impression she longed for home. The yards people all returned to their normal activities.

Murphy looked across and caught the eye of Nellie. He hadn't seen her there before. He was bracing himself for the approach. Getting up the bravado to shield against any humiliation of a rejection, should he receive one! Only time will tell. Over with you and ask her out. He stepped towards her.

Mick "Horse" Flanagan had clocked her way earlier than Johnny. He advanced to her and engaged in a wee bit of the chat. Did she enjoy the show? Did she want to see some more? She was curious as to the ways of the place, so she accepted the tour. They walked away together. Johnny played at mucking out a stable nearby. From there he and the whole yard heard a scream.

Johnny ran towards the sound. It was coming from a cranny between two detached stables at the far end of the yard. A few others were seconds behind him. They got there, just in time to see him drop the bloodied spading fork. Johnny was trying to quickly protect Nellie's dignity, at the same time. She was on the ground, a quivering mess of emotions, blubbering, "I said No." The Guards were called. So was the doctor, who wasted no time for it was an undertaker's labour required, not his own. He quipped without checking himself that the fork surely put a stop to Flanagan's intumescent behaviour. Mercifully he turned to Nellie and suggested he examine her at his surgery. She thanked him but, in reality, she just couldn't face another man being intimately aware of her. Not today, not ever.

GET AWAY DRIVING
2023

Inside the van an equally incredible scene as the baby in the car park was unfolding. Jack was lying at first on the woman. She was screaming and struggling, raising an almighty hue and cry. Subconsciously in an instant she surveyed her situation. She was bundled into a van by a man in a sheepskin coat forcefully. The van was hurriedly exiting the car park. She considered herself abducted. She was afraid. When in Ireland in the 2020's this happened, there can only be one outcome - rape, death, and disappearance. She certainly had cause to be very afraid right now and so she was!

"Get off me," she screamed. Jack was obligingly doing so. This confused her. "Please don't hurt me," she pleaded weakly. The strength was literally seeping from her voice box. "Please let me go .... I'll tell no one."

"Madam, I'm most terribly sorry," Jack started to apologise, to reassure her he had no intention to harm her. Of course, yes, absolutely they would let her go. They just needed to find a safe place to pullover and let her out. An unoccupied curbside loading bay, common now in areas of urban sprawl, presented itself as a good place to do this. They dutifully pulled in, eager to offload the uninvited guest and re-commence their *flawless getaway.*

Tamsin was numb now from the overload going on in her brain. She was surprised to be now free of her captors. Her son now flashed again into her mind. She needed to get back to him immediately in the car park. This distracted her enough to not take in the van license plate although she tried for sure. She was only a five-minute walk back to the car park. She would ring the guards whilst running. Where was her phone? She realised she had left it in the buggy bag. This made her run as hard as she could. She never thought to ask a passerby for help. She just moved as fast as she could pushing and flailing at people. She shouted to get them out of her way. To those about the place she would have seemed quite mad. She didn't care and in truth she probably was. Of far more importance right then was reuniting with her son. They had been apart only a short spell, but it seemed to her an eternity. She needed to find him.

On re-entering the car park, she saw no one. Her little boy was now missing. The thugs who took him also nowhere to be seen. Neither was the buggy which had her phone within it. She just crumpled on the concrete driveway, flooding her immediate vicinity in her own tears. People circled her to offer help. She ranted dementedly of abductions of her and now her child. A Samaritan rang 112 for her although she was too distraught to be aware of this.

The same van that had just swallowed her whole returned and pulled up close. The windows down, Jack called loudly. "Excuse me miss. I know where your baby is. I'd like to help you get it back." Some of the bystanders felt involved and went to protect the woman by moving toward the van. Timmy saw this and grabbed a bar he kept under his seat and jumped out swinging it at people like a Jedi knight in training. As he did, he walked over to Tamsin who was startled by the latest developments. Jack was still within the van. From the open window, as loud as Jack could without a tannoy, he said, "We do not have your baby. We were being chased by bad people who took your son when chasing us. We have something they want. We can help you get the baby back. We can't deal with police so please …. come now!" Tamsin was now unable to think clearly. Her autopilot engaged, she got up and went towards the van. Jack told Tamsin he would slide into the back so Tamsin could sit up front. Jack realised the back would be a scary place for her and complied himself with his own instructions. As they were all aboard, Jack begged Timmy to go, to drive them away from there.

So, the three unlikely amigos were in the moving van. Timmy had asked where he should go. Jack had said best to go to the bolt hole. This was a nickname he used for a temporary hiding place he would set up in the geographical area of a sting. He had organised one in Limerick simply because of the size of the operation. As he only lived in actuality an hour away, he never expected to have to use it. It was a student flat over a hairdresser off the Ennis Road. It was basic amenity wise, bleak in fact, but it was for emergency use only. This was starting to feel like an emergency.

5 MINS BEFORE

The con was at last getting back on track. They were now rid of the problem of the unwanted sidekick in the back of the van. She'd hopefully be calming down now as she was free of them too. In fairness the chaps had to admit the woman was just as badly inconvenienced by events as they were. Timmy and Jack's mutual blood pressure was stratospheric but starting to fall to normality with the woman gone. The money was transferred and that was something to be grateful for.

However, the time to breathe and reflect brought Jack a realisation hard to avoid. The whole operation was turning out to be a monumental anticippointment. Whose fault? It was Timmy who mixed in the traders into this. That's when it soured. Once the elements of each universe seeped into one another, chaos was inevitable. He could not hold it in any longer. "This whole thing is a total nightmare. Why did you have to do the clothes deal today?" Timmy could tell Jack was not in a debating mood. He decided that he needed to be contrite with a side of grovel. "Jack, I'm sorry, super sorry that I messed up." Jack was not ready to forgive. He was about to serve another verbal volley when his phone beeped alerting him of an incoming text.

IF YOU WANT CHILD TO LIVE RING ME BEFORE 4 TODAY

"Cohen has that woman's baby. She will definitely go to the cops. This will be over. We need time." "Now hang on," came the reply. Shamefully the two debated this news. Both being a sort of devil's advocate. Both musing how this had nothing to do with them. They could now be away on their toes and scarper.

Jack, becoming more controlled again, told Timmy to go back to the car park. Damage control had to be the name of the game from now on. Or maybe, just maybe Jack's conscience wouldn't allow a little one to suffer because of him.

SHOW & TELL
1960

Ivan the terrible, as his masonic friends called him, stood behind and slightly to the left, of his very, ex-girlfriend turned holy woman. She had taken him on a bit of a tour of the place mostly in silence. When she talked it was mostly a pleasantry to the past. She never explained what she planned to show him or how it would help him.

They had come to a darkened corridor in which he could feel a draught. He was guessing the door before him was a cellar of some type. Dymphna, or Mother Superior to you and me, then finally spoke up.

"What I'm about to show you is known by so, so few .... It's a secret. I was not aware this problem even existed until I became management. The shop floor girls (the nuns of lower rank) are largely unaware of what is in there. Only those that need to know .... know."

"So, why do I need to know?" he asked impatiently. She turned to face him. She explained as she had upstairs, that money was scarce. But if a problem is genuinely solved, she was sure the convent would pay. She unlocked the door with a huge, oversized crude metal key which was probably the original key from when the place was built. The heavy door opened slowly, creaking as it went. Not so scary to open such a door when you have back up. They went inside a dark room and flicked on the electrical light. The room brightened up in a yellowy hue.

Once illuminated it took a second for Ivan's eyes to adjust. Metal and wooden shelves that were full of dust from minimal use were what he saw. Every so often he saw they had a tightly wrapped hessian bundle on them. He counted maybe twelve or so. He wasn't sure but the wrapping seemed to be recycled from coal bags.

Dymphna explained that sometimes when babies came to the ladies they helped, they were often illegitimate. Some of those due to complications didn't make it full term. Someone was giving the girls a second chance. They can pretend it never happened and go on in life happier and wiser. But only if no record exists of the child. They, in each convent, had to come up with imaginative ways to make that happen. This convent had been ignoring the problem until she came. It was quite a blow to her sense of Christianity that this was one of the first problems she had to sort. But tackling it effectively would surely earn her serious kudos with the top brass.

"You see, we have three convents in this diocese. I imagine when word spreads that I have found this unfortunate problem a solid dependable workable solution, I'm sure you would be able to obtain retainers."

What she asked of him repulsed him. He certainly would never think of himself as a monster capable of these things. Yet, desperate times call for desperate measures. And he was desperate. The question was, was he desperate enough?

CLEAN UP TIME
2023

"So, where is my baby?" Tamsin said. Jack replied all questions would be answered, but first he had essential tasks to perform. He ordered Timmy to ring MJ to burn HQ and evacuate to the bolt hole. The home office had all the plans on the board for today. To burn meant destroying that stuff. The only other incriminating information was on laptops. They used cloud storage on the dark web. Encrypted, of course, but leaving the laptops gave the guards an easy start. She had to do it within the next hour.

Next, he told Timmy and Tamsin to hand over their phones. He took down Cohen's number from his phone (scribbling it on a pocket scrap as you do) and put the three of them in a bag. To get to the flat they used a traffic bridge to cross the Shannon with a footpath along each edge. The traffic was slow, so Jack jumped out the side door and looked over the wall to make sure the way was clear. Imagine how infuriating it would be, having thrown these links to them away, if they floated river ward only to land on some passing Popeye type below.

That socially minded citizen could then claim a reward on Crime Line and stitch them right up. Nothing below so not going to happen! He then threw the handsets into the drink.

The concrete road took them through suburban Limerick. On arriving at their destination, they turned in, crossing the footpath, and stopping safely on the tarmac island car park in front of a few corner shops, one of which was the bolt hole.

UTOPIAN MIRAGE
1975

So, Nellie was a survivor. She and her new husband Tom Delaney had plans. They would have a family. There's a thought - she would be a mum again. Who would have ever thought she would want that? Especially after her annus horibillus, the 1963 abominations against her. But no matter, things would keep improving for Mrs. Nellie Delaney. She sat in her kitchen drinking tea with her beloved, listening to Gaybo on the radio. Tom was home for lunch. He was fretting over her as she was expecting again. She was so happy, life was healing her, she was moving on.

The radio paused one of Gaybo's thought provoking discussions for the news. ("We bring breaking news this hour of the death of an inmate at Portlaoise Prison. The prisoner was said to have been distraught after receiving some mail and hung himself. A full investigation is under way…")

Nellie erupted emotionally throwing herself to the floor. She didn't want poor Johnny to suffer as he had or to end as he had. She had been as gentle as she could. Her letter had a paragraph on the sale of the yard by the family trying to salvage something from the "Horses'" empire now in ashes around them. More chit and chat and local gossip and passed on sympathies from everyone. Ah shur, the whole community was on his side. If any reporters came asking about the affair, everyone unitedly blanked them. Nothing to see here, leave us alone.

The letter rested on the floor underneath him hanging. The guards remained tight-lipped officially on the situation. But one reporter bought a guard a scoop or two. He was rewarded by the quote: "It wasn't the rope, for that lad died of a broken heart."

24/7/75
Johnny Murphy Prisoner
Portlaoise Prison, Portlaoise.

Nellie Delaney
Priory Park
BallyGortMore
Tipperary

Dear Johnny,

Tis Nellie here.

………………………………………………………………………………………………………
……………………………………………………………..

Again I want to say how very sorry I am for what has
happened to you. You heard me tell the Judge why you did
it. I can't understand why he has put you there. You don't
deserve it.

Johnny, as sad as I am. I must build a life. They took my
baby. Flanagan took my respectability. Yes, they all felt
sorry for me but still viewed me as damaged. I just want
to live. I'm sorry but I've got married. He's a good man.

I will never forget what you did. You will always have my
heart because of it.
Be well xxx. Ne

Ps I will write to you from time to time if acceptable. My
debt to you, I can never repay it.

135

BABIES DAY OUT
2023

Little Dylan was surrounded earlier by the burly traders. Hennessy Snr had picked up the orange soother a space and a half away. Its florescence ensuring he noticed it in a search prompted by Callanan, who knew just enough on the subject to be aware kids came equipped with pacifiers nowadays. Once retrieved, a quick hand manoeuvre to flick off the fresh grit from its rubbery protrusion, then he pushed it into the screaming child's face like a cartoon cream pie. Two maybe three sucks later, he stopped crying. They walked him towards Guild's bar to meet their new employer.

On their return one of the lads had to open the bar door ahead of the one steering the buggy. It was just as well that it was a rugged piece of kit, as he pushed young Dylan as if he was strapped into a sack trolley, for immediate delivery to Guild's cold room out back. The glass crunch was loudly unpleasing. Some nodules became embedded in the lad's boots. They nervously updated Cohen. They handed over the baby.

It's true we are all human. Many hard men had soft human
sides. Even Hitler went on romantic breaks away for
weekends with Eva Braun to the Eagles Nest in the
Bavarian Alps. From this you might imagine Aidan Cohen
softening on seeing baby Dylan. He didn't. "Desiree. This
glass will need cleaning up. Then mind this baby." He
texted the man whom he now knew to be a thief. Perhaps
the thieving git would have a crisis of conscience when he
knew what was at stake, he hoped.

Desiree heard the command. She felt now like a World War
One weary soldier about to go over the top. She grabbed
her broom and dustpan and a small bin from behind the bar.

The two baby-less traders instinctively wanted to look busy
and so voluntarily picked up the up turned table and righted
it. Number three was taking his paternal role quite seriously
now. This manifested itself in his rocking the buggy
whenever Dylan threatened noise.

As Desiree swept up the glass and shoveled it bin wards
she did as any cleaner doing monotonous work would do.
She daydreamed.

She couldn't have children. A bad miscarriage broke her emotionally. Then cancer was discovered in her uterus. So out it came. She still remembers the doctor explaining things to her. The upshot was she would be healthy and live a long happy life but would be unable to conceive. It was a few years ago now, but it was no easier.

And here she was like the Pharaoh's wife's, lady in waiting, from the Bible account of Moses, being asked to mind another mother's child. Except that woman in the Bible really was Moses' mum. Desiree had no such claim on baby. All the years suppressing her desire to be with child and yet here one turns up as if by mail-order. This was a very surreal situation.

She tentatively approached the babs and saw the journey and the rocking had sent Dylan to sleep. "Mr. Cohen, the child is asleep. Can I pop to shops to get him some food and nappies and such?" she asked.

"Get a few euro from the till there and get a bit. Good idea. Don't want to damage the leverage." Cohen in mercy was still transactional in his thinking. "Not much mind. He won't by ours long." Desiree took a fifty as instructed and headed for the door.

TIMEOUT

"Timmy, do the needful!" Jack said, swiveling his head from Tim to the apartment entrance door. Timmy left the van and tentatively entered the door to the stairs of the upstairs accommodations. He continued nervously on the reconnoiter.

Tamsin was still in shock, very mixed up and getting desperate. "It's not too late to finish this. Just help me to get Dylan back." She looked nowhere whilst deciding her next move. Having thought it through she put her hand across on Jack's leg, her fingers pointing around his leg towards the zone. "I'll do anything, just help me ....
Please!"

Timmy's head popped back out the door. "It's clear! Are you coming?" Jack nodded and gestured in the affirmative. He looked into Tamsin's worried eyes and said they would get the child back. She needed to trust him. So, like two holiday goers checking in to an Airbnb, they followed Timmy inside. Her discombobulation returned again when she got the smell of sick off Jack. "I can explain all upstairs," Jack reassured her.

Timmy had already got the kettle going. A brew might allow everyone some time for contemplation; and who wouldn't welcome some of that on what has turned out to be one of the most stress-inducing days of everyone's lives. A full review and assessment session couldn't properly commence till the arrival of MJ. Many hands make light work. There is wisdom in a multitude of counsellors. Jack recalled these pearls of wisdom mentally, as he decided to wait for her. Anyway, he had more pressing issues. For instance, the hormonal woman in his charge. It was also nagging at him that his own personal car was sitting at Fill Up Again's.

First things first. He turned to the woman. "Please sit down. I'll be mother! We need to have a long talk." He who had a liking for language, listened to a podcast on the use of language; on this he had heard a new phrase to him, although it was a very old and now out of fashion. To bitch the pot, meaning to make the tea and have a catch up whilst so doing. Raconteur Jack would love to have informed his

audience of its appropriateness despite its seeming rude.
Yet he didn't.

"Right. Obviously, you are wanting to know what's going
on. My name is Jack, that's Timmy, MJ will soon join us."
No sense in worrying over covers now. It was well blown.
"We were doing a con on a very bad man. It went wrong so
we had to run. We "met" you and here we are, Miss! Ah,
what do I …? Can I … call you?"

"Tamsin," came the reply. "Look, just give it back to him,
whatever you stole. He gives you, my Dylan. The poor lad
will beside himself. Please." She looked at him with big
eyes. Given his profession he knew how to emote a
situation. Thinking of charitable ads for example, the little
child always has big eyes staring right at the camera as if at
you directly. It's a tactic to illicit sympathy. As baby
Dylan's theft was very raw for his mother, Jack evaluated
this to be a genuine plea of a distraught mother. "It's
definitely option A. Let me just think awhile. There might
be other ways."

"Other ways, other ways, I'll show you other ways." She
jumped at Jack knocking over the teacups and breaking

them. She clawed him with her female talons. Surely only a guitar plucker would need nails that long. Timmy came over and pulled her off him. "Steady," he warned.

As Jack straightened himself, Timmy pushed Tamsin back into an armchair. She was crying, "Dylan …. Dylan."

Jack suddenly felt the need for female allies. Where was MJ? He pulled out some fresh burner phones, from some dresser drawers and started to set them up. He looked at his watch which he had not done for a while now. It read 1.43pm.

Timmy decided he would go to the shops to fetch some milk and maybe some pasta in case they spent the night. He offered to fetch Jack's car from Fill Up Again's whilst out.

Jack told him OK but to hurry back. They needed to all discuss the way forward. Tamsin was starting to worry rightly that this wasn't going to be over by this afternoon. Mind you, so was Jack. Where the flip was MJ?

NEAR MISSES

MJ had heard what the boss wanted. So here she was, having parked on the road out front looking at the office door. She had a key and permission to enter to retrieve the laptops and papers from the planning stage. She still felt nervous like she was breaking and entering. Perhaps it was the fact that being caught with the laptops etc. would clearly link her with the fraud. After looking around she let herself in. She stepped over the mail, grabbed what she came for and then on her way out she picked up the post. It was the usual, bills and a few circulars including a letter with the ancestry stamp on it. She thought, "Why is everybody so interested in the past?"

There was certainly nothing nostalgic in her past worth hanging on to; no good times she could wax lyrically on. She popped the post into one of the laptop bags. Having relocked the door, she started to walk away from the office. Suddenly a G class pulled in the drive. It was Finley, Cohen's right arm at the wheel. "Sorry, anyone inside?" he asked. She just shook her head, grunted, "No," and walked onwards. She was grabbed by the arm and forcefully pulled back to face Finley. As she looked into his eyes, he said he was sorry, but he really needed to talk to Delaney. Did she know where he might be? Her arm was sore from the strength of the grab at her. She felt nothing, she heard nothing. She wasn't in the present; she was trapped in her past. It was her drunk dad she saw. It was his voice she heard. She was that frightened little girl again, just surviving. Her antiperspirant was failing.

Thinking on her feet she replied, "No and I really needed to talk to him, too. He sold me a job lot of detergent. It's useless, causes colours to run." By pretending to want him this way she hoped to be let go. It worked. Finley had a thought for a second, gave her a card and asked if she would ring him if she found Jack. He too needed to speak with the chap urgently. He was sorry for the rough treatment, but he had a job to do. Why are they always sorry after? Like that makes up for the trauma and emotional damage they do.

She jumped in her car and drove away leaving Finley having a snoop at the house. He rang Limerick to advise the boss that Jack was not yet home.

MJ drove a good five to ten miles away. She professionally checked if she was being followed or not, then pulled over. She grabbed the wheel with both hands, rested her head on same and cried. And cried. She had much to process. When she started to recover, she thought she deserved a raise. "Jack should be paying me danger money," she concluded.

At more or less the same time, Timmy was taking a short cut through the babies supply section. Desiree was there, frustrating herself greatly. She had some nappies but was looking along the shelf for the right age, milk formula.

Having spotted what she hoped was the right one, she couldn't quite reach it. Timmy noticed this as he passed. He helpfully grabbed at it and handed the container to a grateful mother eager to get on with her day. Their singular minute degree of separation was amplified by the fact that they had unwittingly parked, facing each other in the car park.

If only the two were aware of their forced connection. Then these torrid times could be massively improved upon. But that was not to be. They moved on to complete their shopping quests as passing ships in a fog.

Timmy was a little giddy. He was now the owner of a lot of money. And as he crossed the car park on the way back to his motor, he saw it, the bookies shop. In he went, to the wall of TV screens. He looked around as the sensory overload reminded him of why he liked to gamble. A dog meeting, three different horse races and a cycling race all competed for his undivided attention. The noise of punters consuming the sports red tops one page at a time. And turn the page, read, dismiss and turn the page.

He actually recognised one of the names on the horses. "Childer." She has a decent track record, some great form. He had read a bit of the red top banter on her earlier in the juice bar. He had the money to invest. He fancied this. His adrenaline was starting to flow. He approached the counter for the first time in years. "One hundred thousand on Childer." The rush was amazing. The counter staff, who were obliged to do as trained, signaled the owner to approve the outlandish bet. Their mouths wide open with the shock of hearing such an unusual bet. They were used to dole spenders spending maybe five or ten pounds; even GAA boys spending a few hundred as their habits grew. This wasn't that. "What do you know that we don't?" he asked Timmy. This was a rhetorical question posed by the manager so as to give him time to speak to the boss man. "Nothing," was Timmy's reply. "In that case, are you sure? There's no recantation here."

Timmy was quite prepared to meet the consequences. The boss man checked his data base and saw Timmy McGuire's name on a troubling gamblers list. All listings were ancient. So, McGuire was a reformed gambler who was now falling off the wagon. This would be easy then, like taking candy off a baby. On the other hand, it was the case that McGuire was scamming somehow. That sort of thing was for a movie or book or suchlike. No, this chap was just an unlucky rusty lapsed gambler back for another go. The bet was accepted, the slip filled in accordingly.

The horses were skittish by the starting tape. The commentator had just been handed over the airwaves and was ready to go himself.

"They are at this moment pacing to the line to start The Sequoia Cleaning 1½ mile Hurdle. The starter has dropped the tape and they're off!"

NEW ARRIVALS
1963

The Morris Minor came over the noise producing cattle grid. It then crawled up the gravel drive. The slow crunching of pebbles was bothersome under the four wheels, with their silver plate sized hubcaps. This was a noise Nellie would grow to associate with this moment, forever more, Amen.

The building grew immensely large, grotesquely so, as they got closer to it. Gleamy House was a convent facility. Its job normally was to assist the community in which it stood, by prayers and charitable work where possible. Its occupants, did, in fairness, take this seriously. They would distribute food from their extensive gardens to the poorer members of BallyGortMore.

Whilst it was not normally in the business of wayward women or uncared for children; and yet there was always a couple who needed urgent intervention. This time, its help was sought by the PP who wanted to help the family. The poor girl didn't deserve this.

Had she been truly wayward she would have been for a more institutional home up the country; sending her here was meant as a kindness.

She would help the nuns with some chores befitting her condition till she couldn't. This would pay for them to help with the delivery and rehome the child.

(I'm drawn to Magdalen Laundries by Mary Coughlan for the soundtrack.)

Nellie was conflicted about this a fair bit. Sometimes overwhelmed and looking forward to being rid. Alternatively, as often though, the maternal won out and she would imagine a family of two and how it would work. Stood there in front of the main door at 21 years old, she still thought that "its oakness" was at least 3-4 foot taller than her. When it opened a stern looking woman in black answered the door. She told Nellie to say a proper goodbye as she would not see any kin again till after the delivery.

The parents said she should write them often. Just a couple of minutes later the door was closing, with them outside in a bit of a state.

The nun said to follow her. She did, along the marble floors green around the edges, a yellow sea in the middle with shards of multicolor throughout, up two stairs and down another corridor. She struggled to navigate the steps with her tiny suitcase containing clothes in one hand and in the other a small box of treats. Nothing grand, just a bit of chocolate, some personal toiletries, some writing paper, a freshly filled ink cartridge and pen. Then of course, special, only to her, a few strands of straw that transferred off Johnny Murphy's jacket on that fateful day, onto her dress. She, although in shock as they took him away, knew its significance as a keep sake. Before coming she had crafted a little cloth bag to store it, to protect it as a solid tangible link to her lost love.

As you would expect, icons of Mary and Jesus looked down on her from everywhere. They finally arrived at her digs. She had to share with two other girls, who were both inside the room messing about, giggling and such but came to a sudden silent attention on the nuns entrance. "Tea at 6.

Mass at 7. Bed at 8. Early start in the morning and Mother
Superior will induct you after breakfast tomorrow." "Yes
Miss, I mean Ma'am, I mean, I mean Sister." This set off
the giggle twins again, but the nun already leaving the
room didn't care. "What did you do?" asked one of the
girls. The other looked apologetically at Nellie of rounded
belly. Then to her roomie she said, "She's preggers,
dosey!"

Over the next short while, the 3 became good friends.
Sneaky snacky late night raids on the kitchen,
insubordinate giggle fests on their penguin captors.
Covering for one another, when the nuns version of the
special branch tried to catch them out for these infractions
or when one of them couldn't do their chores because of
their mutual and yet individual conditions.

They were all at different stages and gradually they
laboured in birth and thus were released back to the world
from whence they came. As this was not a mother and baby
home in the strictest sense of the title, it did not follow that
these girls would be replaced with a fresh crop, and they
were not. This meant for poor Nellie her last month or so of
incarceration, were particularly lonely. She would fill the

void writing letters home and reading letters from same when she was lucky enough to receive them.

Nellie's day came too. Sister Margaret, one of the kind ones, a definite candidate for some chocolate, was Nellie's shadow. She was escorting Nellie on her chores with one of the other guests they had. Toilets needed cleaning. Nellie was tired and felt like she was going to pop. She bent down to a toilet. AAAAAGGGGH! She did indeed pop. Her waters broke. Another mess in a bathroom but Nell was not going to be the one to clean it up. A huddle of nuns went to work, hot water, towels, the hoisting of legs into stirrups. "Push, breathe. Wow. They are angry words! It's coming! Remember to push, breathe!! It's a boy!"

She would remember that forever after. It's a boy, they said, not *your son*. No one there ever called her a mother. She would confide many years later, how back then, she did not have the words. But now she had, human incubator. More sadness in her life's ledger.

She was there with her legs in the traditional stirrups. Nellie had her head up in parallel to her ankles. Her body shape resembling a capital letter U to anyone looking at her from the bedside. None of the nuns did look though. She wasn't the first girl they would have seen, stirrup-ed. Nor would she be the last. Nothing new or even noteworthy for an experienced nun to comment on. Ladies glow streaming down Nellie's face. Remember horses sweat, men perspire but ladies merely glow! Her self-same face was gone raspberry red from her exertions thus far.

One of the nuns quipped in a matter-of-fact way, that if Nellie was tired, she could rest later. She would have a few more pains to push out the afterbirth. She was struggling to catch her breath, doing loud audible inhale exhale noises. It was as if she was winded after running a marathon.

Suddenly a look of pain returned to her face, a look of constipation. She groaned all the way from her abdomen. The nuns rallied as they recognised the possibilities. The head nun called to her assistants, "Fresh water and towels quickly." Nellie was in tremendous pain and an equal amount of confusion. Why did she feel her body was poised like an active volcano ready to erupt again?

The nuns were assuming the same positions they had for the first delivery. "What's going on?" she screamed. They were stoic and calm. Nun one annunciated, "It appears you are blessed with a second gift for God."

Nellie digested the information, a second child. Amazing. Scary. Immediate! She screamed and heard the nuns say, "Breathe, push, good, again breathe, push, still with the angry words! Breathe, push." Silence. "Waaaaaa waaaaaa waaaaaa." That's baby for hello, I've arrived. Then one of the women in the room, said this time, "It's a girl."

She gave her babies some life-giving milk. She tried to be there for them in other motherly ways. The Order interfered and eventually a showdown occurred. They waved papers she signed at her and said the children would go to a good home. And re-homed they were. She never found out with who! You can believe she tried. She called back to the convent often during those earlier years to see if the wall of silence as to the kids' whereabouts could ever be breached. She also went about asking the state for help many times. She asked her local civil servants at the local county office many times for help in their location. The wall she met there was more a wall of brick as opposed to silence. Bureaucracy at its best.

The way the days were structured after; the geography of the Convent itself; the shroud of secrecy maintained by the nuns. These things made it impossible for the new mothers to interfere with the handover of the babies to their new "parents." As the women prepared for their own departures back to normality, they could never be sure if the children were still there or already gone ahead of the mams, to their new lives.

Every criminal gets released one day. The Morris Minor eventually returned, and she heard the pebbles crush again. Would this illicit happiness? She was getting out. No. Just emptiness remained. She would be a husk of her former self, for a long, long, long time to come.

She tried to get her parents to understand her feelings. If they did, they never showed it. They were sincerely hurt for her, but Ireland currently was a very strange place. The Government, even if it wanted, could not educate the people of the place by itself. For many years previous it was the religious orders who provided education to the masses. From 1966 onward the Government set up free secondary education to create an educated workforce to export initially. The hope of course was that industry would kick up and job numbers would grow. But they still needed a big involvement from the religious to make this happen. This meant the religious had become used to not being challenged, to getting their own way. To being respected by the lesser ones like Nellie's parents. She, therefore, was reduced to a shadow of herself and still very much alone despite the support shown by her family and friends.

21/1/63
BallyGortMore Convent
of the Immaculates.
BallyGortMore
Co. Tipperary

Mr & Mrs Madigan
Stud Farm Lane
BallyGortMore
Tipperary

Dear Mam and Dad

We are coming up on a month since I came here. How's the farm going? I hope that Dad can manage now he does not have me or Johnny to help him. I keep thinking how depressing our holidays were this year. Will every festive season be spoilt now leaving this horrible time behind us? Can it ever be behind us? These nuns have us up out of bed at stupid o clock. Prayers said and brekkie ate, they find us work to do. One of the nuns keeps saying it's our penance. I keep wondering why am I doing penance? My job this week was to wash up old coal bags! Pointless. Not penance, just punishment.

I've had to say goodbye to Trish. Her baby is here for a week now. It seems a Dublin couple are giving it a good home. Trish overheard their accent when they picked up the babs. She wasn't supposed to be anywhere nearby. She walked the place with a bucket and mop telling any enquirer, she was asked to clean a nearby area of floor. An innocent lie to see her baby off. She herself went the next day. She had a final night with me, but she wasn't right after it. I mean how can it be right to split mother and child? Is the family not an important part of being a Christian? Why create so many broken families? I just don't get it.

Don't be mad with me for if I am truthful with you, I am worried about giving up mine. It seems wrong and yet I know how it came about. How could I love such a thing as a forced upon me bastard child?

What must you think of me? You raised a good girl. But I imagine all the women from about, the same who would share a joke with me in the shop. Their gossip must be cruel to endure. I'm sorry to have hurt you.

Perhaps you might send me another choccy bar or two and some more writing paper. I will share the bar with the nicer nuns as a thank you. I love you and miss you so very much. Nels x

Nellie Madigan c/o
BallyGortMore Convent
of the Immaculates
BallyGortMore
Tipperary

To our precious daughter, Ne,

It's the feast of St Brigid herself today. A holy woman who looked after the less well-off of her time. These nuns may struggle to fill her shoes but are they not trying? Of course, they are, be patient with them, girl.

That said, it was lovely to hear from you. We are sorry for all that's happened to you. Your mother and I should have kept a better eye on you. It was our job to protect you. We know we failed you, Ne.

Don't worry at all about the gossip. Most are on our....your side. Any of the real meanies I have threatened I will take my shot gun to. And I will.

Good ol' Johnny stood up for you. He's ever such a good lad. But sweetheart, some battles we just won't win. This is Satanic spawn inside you. Sur what else would it be? the way it happened?

Please understand the priest is sympathetic to us and to you, but only because he thinks we will do the right thing. The church has power like you wouldn't believe. A few words from the pulpit and we'd be outcasts, shunned for a crime we didn't commit. I understand you are divided on the issue. Please don't make trouble, it's for the best.
Táimid brónach,

Dad and Mammy.

Ps chocolate and paper included.

OLD HABITS DIE HARD
2023

"Well, I say they are off, but actually they are still walking, same as before the tape fell. Highly unusual start to a race this. Completely legal but unusual. Where's the advantage in it? I'm not sure. With not much else to talk about, can I just mention I was down by the betting ring earlier. A lot of the bookies were climbing above their leather bags heading for their boards to adjust the odds on Childer. Some serious support being shown for him, it would seem. They remain spread across the width of the track pacing as if they were in a parade ring, not a ra...."

"Greatpretender is the first to break ranks. His jockey jolting him into action. The rest must follow or be left out of it and so they do. But Greatpretender the immediate leader hugs the far rail, two lengths to the good. The field are compacting towards that same rail. Revengeissweet second now to the rear of Greatpretender. The remainder bunch up in a tight formation."

"To put some shape on it, it's Greatpretender, Revengeissweet, Snookered, Itwillbegrand. At the back of the field, we have Nomessin', Childer behind him, joint last with Dogmeat on his outside."

"The track is a righthand bend circuit so nearside to us from the camera is the outside from the field's perspective. Childer is hampered between the rail and Dogmeat. They drift past the view stand and away clockwise along the track."

"As they take this first bend, they are all looking strong, but it remains Greatpretender, Revengeissweet, Snookered, Itwillbegrand, Nomessin', Childer behind him, joint last with Dogmeat on his outside."

The betting shop clientele all started shouting at their selection. Their cheers at this early stage were choral in nature. A roomful of optimists. It was way too early for anything else. They were all glued to the tellys.

"Now they approach the first jump and all look to take it with gusto. Up and over is Greatpretender, a powerful looking animal, she is too. Revengeissweet just clips the hurdle with the right hind hoof landing awkwardly. The jockey marshalling Revengeissweet to wake up and do better but losing ground there to Greatpretender. The gap opens to 4 lengths there."

Some in the betting shop exclaim shock at the Revenge's decline. Timmy did not flinch. He was dispassionate, true, but focused on those moving pixels upon the wall.

"Snookered has drifted wide over the jump. He receives a reminder to race ahead and picks up the pace. Pulling alongside Revengeissweet, Snookered now challenges for second place. Afterwards it's still the flight formation of Itwillbegrand, Nomessin', Childer and Dogmeat still boxing him in."

"The punters favourite now well supported, Childer will have to find a space to race or there will be a lot of littering around the betting ring later."

"Heading up hill on the straight that allows a strong horse to make progress. It's still Greatpretender. Revengeissweet who's not been at it properly since he clipped that first, gives way to Snookered. In fact, he's drifting off there.

Slowing up too. So, he's now passed by the rest. So, it's Greatpretender, Snookered, Itwillbegrand, Nomessin', Childer and Dogmeat still in equal last place."

"Revengeissweet definitely has been pulled up. There's obviously some concern over him since he hit the fence. That's a good call, mitigate the damage and live to fight another day."

Buyer's remorse was descending like a smog at the Revenge's decline. So much so that several punters started leaving the shop for air. Snookered and Greatpretender fans got loud too, compensating for the absentees. Timmy remained a silent observer.

"Meanwhile heading for our next hurdle its Greatpretender holding onto a strong 4 length advantage. Snookered to his rear. No issue for either on jumping the hurdle. Both well clear without incident."

"Itwillbegrand looks good at this stage for third. Nomessin' leads the rear guard, Childer and Dogmeat remain in the cheap seats but jump the hurdle without any hardship."

"So now all safely over hurdle 2. It's Greatpretender, Snookered has narrowed the gap to 2, maybe 3 lengths in second place. For the each wayers, Itwillbegrand also increasing his pace for third. At the back then, in nearly a separate race is, Snookered with Nomessin', Childer and Dogmeat. The jumps are spaced quite differently apart. The distance between the second and third short enough that they are preparing for the third, about now."

"Again no trouble to frontrunners, all jumping well. Greatpretender still leading in front of Snookered and Itwillbegrand. Nomessin' really ran hard and jumped strong there to narrow the gap between the front and back markers. Childer and Dogmeat increase the pace to stay in contention. They jump the third now. Childer happy to increase his speed. But that's not true of Dogmeat who's tumbled. His jockey rolls clear. His silks will need a good soak to get those grass stains out. Horse and rider are alright though. That's all that matters. Childer now sees his chance veers wide looking to move into the fast lane. The jockey waves a reminder."

Of course, the Childer's supporters cheer! Dogmeat's are tearing up their slips. Some had even lost interest in the race, choosing to pick another investment from the next race covered on television. Timmy was consistent in quietness but was cracking a wry smile. Come to papa!

"Now, it's Greatpretender, Snookered, Itwillbegrand. Nomessin' fails to find pace as Childer is on the attack taking fourth place from the uncooperative hood wearer. The space between front and back groups now gone. They form the one decent stampede around the next bend. Keep an eye on the light green, dark green squares, the silks of our fields female jockey as she spurs on her mount now, who is showing serious designs on achieving a place finish. Childer accelerates strongly. It's Nomessin' who is now impeded by the equine traffic jam."

"The front few still allowing the leader Greatpretender to set the pace. The track is moving to a downhill section, but Greatpretender is not gaining ground, just doing enough to hold the lead from Snookered. Then it's Itwillbegrand, Childer still pressuring having overtaken Nomessin' on her outside. As we approach the fourth, its Greatpretender, Snookered a former winner of this race by the way. Followed by Itwillbegrand, Childer and now its Nomessin' becoming irrelevant to the rear."

"Right all jumped the penultimate hurdle safely and surely. One final obstacle then a sprint about the final bend to the post. As they leave the fourth, its Greatpretender holding on. Snookered refusing to quit, Itwillbegrand and Childer inching closer to the leaders. Nomessin' really only jaunting now."

"Itwillbegrand showing ambition. Childer likewise. Wait a minute Itwillbegrand is in trouble. The jockey appeared to lose the foothold in the stirrup. Unbalanced momentarily he lost his whip and is off the pace now. Childer bullies on."

By the volume of cheers meaning both in number and intensity, not to mention the decibel level, Timmy was not the only one hoping in the room. He did wonder how many were only copying him thinking he had a scooby as to the outcome.

"Maybe a half furlong to the final, it's Greatpretender, Snookered, Itwillbegrand now being overtaken by the speed machine that is Childer. Now the lengths gap opens to the rear. Nomessin' just fulfilling the contractual obligations now. Childer's still finding something, that green on green check is growing on me."

The bookies must be nervous. She is here to win.

"That's something to see, Childer is still quickening. The others mount a defense but are running out of gas so approaching the last we have a new leader Childer still in the ascendency. Following not ready to concede, Greatpretender, Snookered, Itwillbegrand and Nomessin'."

"Approaching the final jump now. It's Childer who's pulling ahead of Greatpretender. Snookered going up a gear, she may have to take second place after the jump. Itwillbegrand and Nomessin' both showing signs of tiredness now falling back slowly. Up goes Childer and maybe ¾ length behind, up goes Greatpretender. Now neck and neck with Snookered jumping on the wide line."

"Oh Nooooo. Disaster strikes for Childer. She is slumped over top of the jump. A heart attack possibly. We will tell more as we can. Jockey not hurt but looks shaken up a fair bit."

Timmy's temporary disciples, in the betting shop all reacted loudly. Some had irresponsibly put money on, that would have been better spent on groceries, light and heat, actual living, instead of the dreaming that goes on, in a bet placers head. A mere handful had still an interest in the race. They strained to continue to hear the commentary.

"Itwillbegrand and Nomessin' both stopped up in case of collision with Childer."

"So now in the final sprint, it literally is a two-horse race! And they are both trying their best. They are neck and neck ......and still neck and neck. They power to the finish. A photo one I bet ....Greatpretender and Snookered together across the line."

"Greatpretender pushed the race agenda from the off. Her team will feel cheated if worst happens. Snookered judged well to be so close. Snookered's team would be only the delighted to win this again. And what about poor Childer? The vets now confirming Childer is deceased. More on that from studio."

Timmy was bereft, crestfallen and looking into the floor. His natural reaction to hold his head with his two hands showing his elbows out was similar to many a gambler on a loser. No philosophical responses would soothe him. What a total idiot he truly was!

He now totally used to ducking and diving acted on impulse and left the shop quietly. His instinct to run and hide from the trouble he had inflicted on himself was intense. How could someone so savvy be so stupid? so full of ego?

Meanwhile the shop customers who remained were awaking to the fact that Snookered was on the verge of the double. Those who backed him were going a little loopy at the prospect of collecting winnings.

(Snooker Loopy by Chas & Dave. It would have to be. Post me.)

The manager realised Timmy left and rang the boss. "Go after him then, I want to know where to send the debt collectors." Overhead half the televisions showed the still taken for the photo finish. The blue and white silked jockey obscuring the view of the red silked one almost perfectly. It really was a tight finish.

ASSET EROSION

It was getting very close to the four o'clock deadline. For the past hour or so, Jack had shown his human side to his captive audience. He had made a few cups of tea. They first met with a frosty response. Tamsin didn't know him and what he was capable of! All the while, she kept trying to push getting her son back to her, as the only conversation worth having.

Jack again muted his endless apologies, followed by reassurances that what they had was valuable to Cohen. Whilst he had any chance of getting it back, Dylan would be Ok! And he's very young; He'll not remember a minute of it.

With maybe 15 minutes to spare and within minutes of each other, both MJ and Timmy came back. Timmy had retrieved Jack's actual car and got the groceries. MJ was like, "OMG, that was close, I thought I was so dead, back at HQ. Man, this guy is steamed! We got to get away." Then she started gesturing to emphasise her implied distances. "Away, away. While we still can!" Her reaction was becoming sudorific as her anxiety levels rose. She relived her past with every thought. She didn't want any man to get the opportunity to hurt her again. Cohen seemed capable of it even if it was by proxy.

Jack started to gesture in his own way. Addressing the whole team whilst taking MJ by the arms to reassure her, knowingly and privately. "Shhhhhhsssssh! Move in for a team huddle."

His team obeyed exactly like they do on Superbowl day when the coach sends out a discreet instruction, so the other team can't see it. And yet his team can do the move without the oppositions sufficient interference.

His huddle conference commenced. Suggestions? MJ: "We run far and now!" Timmy: "We got the lotto win; we go into the air." Tamsin looked at the huddle and it was not a good idea for their chat to be confidential. They may be making the wrong choices. She jumped on the huddle, attacking with the viciousness of a pack animal. A hungry pack animal. A distraught mother. Little difference, it would appear.

"You're running! I see it in ye,..they'll kill him. Pleeease!," she appealed as they all again stood upright.

Jack looked at the team and the collateral damage, to try and calm both sides. "We need more time." He dialed Cohen. "Give me back my money, you thieving piece of work." Jack, who needed to soothe Tamsin's motherly apprehension sought assurances before any chat about money.

Cohen had learned of himself in therapy and since then in life, that he was angry over being abandoned. And he got angry over loads of things since. In fairness to him he tried not to be, but it was primal. He called Desiree over. She was holding the baby, literally.

And she was doing a good job too, so baby was quite content. Cohen held the phone up to capture Dylan gurgling. "If you can't hear him, I'd be happy to upset him a bit." Jack quickly again gesturing, "No, no, let's do nothing rash. Right now look, it's all getting a bit out of hand. I know it's crooked money, so all is fair, eh? But you have an innocent there. I want to make this end well for all of us, him included. So here it goes. Mind him. Every hour

he's safe, my techie will send you ½ million. Hurt the
child, we bolt with your money!"

Outside the bolt hole, a guy in a betting shop branded
fleece got off his scooter. He called the boss man with his
location. He was told to wait, a Land Rover discovery full
of capable collection agents (they were persuasive was the
implication), was on the way.

DOING THE FORBIDDEN
1961

Ivan Boswell was 35, that's half his biblically ordained three score and ten, but he had achieved in his life. His arrangement had spread to several convents. They never asked and he never told of the ultimate destination of the "waste materials" at their disposal.

Professionally then, he had made it. Other big hitters were using his haulage and storage services. It would seem it was now his personal life that was unravelling. His wife had become distant. Yet really, he knew deep down it was his fault, this well-intentioned workaholic had given her the wedge she was using to push them apart. Not to mention his resurfacing feelings for Dymphna, the forbidden fruit. For sure, it always seems sweeter.

He had regular visits to the convent to collect for his troubles. This meant he was often alone with the Mother Superior. Many of the nuns would joke behind her back as to what they were doing. But no one living ever saw them do anything inappropriate.

It's a well-used maxim, isn't it? If a tree falls in a forest and there's no one there to hear it, did it really fall? Boswell's missus just assumed it was all business keeping him out on odd nights. Mostly she was right because he could not trust any subordinates with the job at hand. The fewer who knew the better. Although it would be necessary to include her in this secret soon enough.

It doesn't matter who you are, things can catch you out, though. Dymphna dropped a bombshell on him on one visit.

"I'm pregnant." The pair had grown used to covering up things. She took a year's leave of absence. While away on his dollar a child was born. Charlie Boswell would be his heir. Mrs. Boswell was apoplectic at first. But she was having trouble conceiving herself. So much like her husband she saw this as a practical solution to their societal problems. The nun would tell no one. She would never seek custody. Mrs. B would survive this. She may even grow to feel for the child. It wasn't his fault, after all. Spoiler Alert: She didn't.

CREATIVE DESTRUCTION
1963

It was maybe two or three days before Nellie's release from prison as she unkindly regarded it. The new parents arrived to take away with them their joyous bundles. In Nellie's case of twins, the nuns had the discretion of keeping the pair together or separating them. In reality, not to sound callous, it was market forces that decided it. If a suitable couple presented looking to take twins, great. If not, the unattached are dispatched to a suitable candidate in the singular. What was most important, was that the suitable candidate would raise a good God fearing Catholic. At that moment, that's where the demand was, for the singular. A stand-alone instant baby to make a family complete.

To be fair again, the nuns always explained it was a twin and showed off the sibling to the perspectives. It was for compassionate reasons and practical too. To place the two together meant companionship for the pair, but it also meant a larger donation from the couple to the cause. This would always be welcome as it meant that the nuns had more resources to keep up the good work. These resources were necessary. The government contributions were small enough. These were essential services in today's Ireland and if the State wasn't up to it, then the Religious would have to fill the breach.

To minimise the fuss on the day, the actual mother was never informed that today was the day. In many cases the new parents would come and go carrying their new luggage without being noticed at all. They obviously entered the same way Nellie did, up the long drive and through the tall imposing doors into the ornate entrance hall. On the actual day, the birth mothers were all encouraged to do their assigned work as normal. This may have been a lighter load of work, reflecting their weaker state, but it would be enough to occupy them often in some far-off corner of the Convent grounds.

The new parent perspectives would be brought into the Mother Superiors drawing room. After being served tea and a brief chat the junior nuns would bring in the babies to show off. On Nellie's kiddies' day, to give the twins a chance, two cradles were already in the room so when the parents walked in the predictable happened. The mothers' emotions played havoc, her sympathy for the two was strong. However, he was always a more pragmatic fellow, thinking of the money amongst other considerations. What happens next was always a coin toss? But the next few minutes would decide if one or two children left that day.

The mother was looking down on the two semi-content children. She had a hand on each baby blanket. Her eyes were wide. Her heart melting into the possibility. She understood suffering. She was but a youngster herself, when her parents fled west, away from the autocratic bloc that mainland Europe was becoming. She was lucky. They left early enough to avoid the excesses of the war. But she understood displacement. And she even could empathise from a childlike perspective.

"Amran, how can you be hard to the bubbelehs? They surely need our help!" "Shira, please don't try to make me a bad guy. We can't afford to keep two. You know this."

"May Hashem be praised if we can do a good deed. Look at them Amran," said the compassionate Jewess. She knew Gods name as did he, from many a holy writing to be YHWH pronounced Yahweh or JHVH pronounced Jehovah. It seemed to depend on which part of the world you came from as to which you used. Why she couldn't use it, she didn't understand. She knew officially it was because it is too holy. But she knew the other showers used it. As a lover of literature, she visited the church of Jonathan Swift in inner city Dublin and saw it there in the ceiling. So if OK for the others, why not her crowd?

In the same way, Shira was often annoyed by her hubbies overly Jewish attitudes to things and yet he persisted. "I'm sorry. We will take the boy and give him a future and maybe, he will feed us when we are feeble," came the reply. "But I could teach her, she may marry well," she said, trying as hard as she could to be a positive advocate.

"No." It was bad enough to have taken a grilling from the nuns about how these children should only go to fellows of the faith. Now his wife was moral bashing him. He was having none (nun, a cheesy pun opportunity should not be missed, should it?) of it.

Shira at times in life and this was one of those, just didn't quite believe. If Hashem / God whatever name you gave him existed then why in all that's holy, did kids like her, like these tiny innocents suffer so? People of all faith can wrangle in this way. In other faiths she may be described as lapsed. But that was not strictly true for the very sense of justice for the poor, needy and wanting that she easily, naturally displayed, is enshrined in the Mosaic law that she sometimes struggled with. And so here she was fighting for the unknown because she had to, she was morally bound to. Was it a basic humanity of hers or religious programming still within her? These were questions for another time. Now she just listened to her husband.

"We can only afford two thousand pounds for the one child. Where would you have me find four?" As he said this he stared at his wife, yes but also the Mother Superior. "She's charging a lot and why so much? It is because we are Jews. Yes, she thinks of us as monied and wants to...."

Mother Superior jumped out of her seat. "It is not because you are Jews, no, simply not Catholic. I admit to those without our faith, we charge more. But I assure you it's to incentivise the faithful, not penalise you."

To strengthen his negotiation, he took his wife's arm. "Shira, this boy will be your son. You will make a great

mother. Now let us take the child to our new Kimmage
home and see can we build a life together, he and we?"
The mum in waiting gave in. The necessary outstanding
paperwork was signed, over tea and sandwiches. Only then
did he drop the carpet bag on the table in front of the
attentive nun. Package collected they left the way they
arrived. It really was a mystery as to why more girls never
saw this activity. Although that said, Nellie was the last of
her dormitory left. On this particular occasion she was
being occupied by the nuns in the orchards at the rear of the
convent. So not likely to see the boy's departure.

**(At scenes end, how about I Fought the Law by The
Clash just for Shira and Nellie too, of course.)**

Mother Superior waited till her clients had left. Sitting in
her desk she felt the pain of a mother. Looking at the
remaining infant in her crib, she wondered how her own
child was doing. She knew well enough as she saw him at
mass with his parents. She had thought to be so near would
help her, but no it reminded her of the pain, this pain of
separation. Tears were secreted. A sense of loss remained
in her as it did Nellie. Yes, Nellie, of all people should

understand how she feels. She certainly now understood Nellie but couldn't show it. A knock on her door and a junior nun entered to fetch the bábóg. A stern, stoic Mother Superior watched its removal.

CHILD MINDER
2023

Cohen was a good bit more satisfied, after the call. He would mind the merchandise and overnight he'd have returned maybe 10 million. Meanwhile he would find the chancers and squash them.

His parents told him stories of their ancestors in Europe who had nothing but strife. He could not let it happen to him. He remembered playing with his Father who taught him to count using a multi-coloured abacus. This reminded him his parents were gone, car crash victims. Life was unfair to him, it had to be said. "Focus don't wallow," he told himself.

Cohen announced, "The child may need minding overnight. So, close up the bar, please. You're a mum for the night." Desiree gathered herself to close the bar as expediently as she could.

Dylan was getting frustrated at being in the buggy for so long. The noise he was making could annoy the fragile mood of Cohen whose volatility could be relied on. Desiree felt a maternal urge to take him home, away from this war zone.

She wrapped him up and rolled him on out the door. She was doing good here in serving this boy as she was. But she felt on edge as she queued for a bus. What if someone recognised him? Would she be done for kidnapping? On the bus she just looked into his little innocent baby eyes. The poor babs!

Her first thought looking at the poor gossoon, was sadness that this was just a short-term arrangement. This instant family extension was a dream come true for her. Then the guilt kicked in. How must the poor mother feel? Desiree would not like to be in her high heels that's for sure.

When she got home, her hubby had the chips on. On hearing her enter the house, he came from the kitchen saying if she could put the pizza on? His jaw dropped when he saw the buggy. "Des, that's a baby." He pointed at you know what. "Why …Who?" He looked like a puzzle in need of solving. "Let me sort little man out. Then I'll explain," she promised, as she picked up the little man and

gently swayed him on her shoulder. And that was just a
preamble, she then stripped him, got some talcum powder,
a dollop of sudocrem, a new nappy and a new babygro.
When all done the nipper smelled fresh and felt soft. She
laid him out upon a really fluffy rug and ate some pizza and
told her husband what she could, which was the baby was
found at work, she agreed to mind it, at least for tonight so
the search for the parents could be completed.

And that's what she did. That whole evening, she played
patta-cake, sang nursery rhymes, fed bottles. She had
enough stuff logistically. Her child's unused nursery was
upstairs fully equipped, left as a shrine to what would not
be. So, baby Dylan even had a crib to sleep in as he wanted
to.

Desiree's husband had questions about how it all happened.
But he saw her interacting with the child. He saw the glint
returning to her eye. He saw life return to her in a way he
had not seen for a very long time. Yes, it was painful to
return to the nursery, the first few times she sought bits and
bobs. The sadness of the loss, previous and personal as it
was, returned in the form of a foggy expression on her face.
A wistful holding of a baby blanky to her face. An isolated

tear or two fell down her cheek. Not really a cry just a sprinkle, anyway as the night wore on her mood lifted. She inhabited her role as mum without any hesitation. Hubby looked on and saw her transform literally before him. She was metamorphising in front of him from husk of former mum to super mum. It was a reaffirming experience for the both of them.

Many, many years earlier Nellie had also served her time as a childminder. Mrs. Boswell had a touch of the post-natal depression. She didn't want owt to do with her wee one, Charlie. Nellie answered an advert in the local paper The BallyGortMore Bullhorn. It was in the situations vacant column. Ivan interviewed her and he hired her immediately. She minded Charlie for years as one of her own. Charlie and Jack knew they were not brothers. That did not matter. They played together, ate and even sometimes Charlie was kept for sleepovers. Charlie served as the big brother Jack never had. Anyone would think Mrs. Boswell really didn't like having him around.

A MULTITUDE OF COUNSELLERS
1971

Nellie walked up the grand steps of the county offices. It was an irony, obvious only to her, apparently that the offices with oversight of adoptions, that had stonewalled her every attempt to reunite with her twins, was also where she now had to come, for state funded trauma counselling.

She truthfully found it hard to be her best self, to embrace the help offered. She had tried so hard on the other side of the building, but no ground was given. The despair amplified to dangerous with each visit now. Her counsellor had decided today, he would be even more callous.

"Right, Helen, how have you been?"

"Angry, sad…. helpless," she replied. "Well, you are coming here awhile now. I think you need to try a bit harder, don't you Helen?"

"My name is Nellie, I for the umpteenth time am Nellie. Helen is probably what will go on my gravestone, I'll give you that, but I am Nellie." She no longer had any control of her life. So at least allow her to be called as she wanted.

"Right sorry, sorry. Nellie. Look I'm running out of options. If you don't improve, I will have to recommend, you are admitted to a lunatic asylum."

Nellie heard that statement and wanted to burst out crying. Fear stopped her and went on stopping her, from ever showing her emotions publicly again. From now on she would function as they wanted. She would be a pleasant member of society. Maybe meet a husband and have more kids just to show them.

The counsellor that day, was very smug, after. She had finally listened and was motivated to change. But the truth was any changes were for appearances sake. It was a hollow victory at best.

(For the film, when they make it, Ashes, I'm Fine would be a perfect soundtrack for poor Nellie here. Don't forget to post me your choices @nellieskids1...I really would love to know.)

2022

Sixty years later, people were still attending this building, feeling broken and at wits end. Desiree Moloney after a session, left the place to head to the pharmacy. The cancer was after taking her only chance at happiness. This was a new blow. The counsellor shifted in his corduroy trousers, shuffling the brown cardboard file covers on his lap. Each had a patient's medical history. The fact that he had so many in this one shift and every shift, told him something better must be done. And yet he did the same as always; "Let's up the dose from 75 to 100mg. At least for 6 months till you can see the sun again." Both women, numbed of pain, but in no way cured.

Pain is universal in nature. It can manifest in the male of the species too.

1983

And so, it was with Aidan Cohen, who realised a short while after that house eviction that the kind of revenge he had executed would not ease his pain. His counsellor tried a form of therapy involving the marshalling of the pain within and trying to exhale it literally. The counsellor tried, with soothing music, to draw pain out of him by using his hands on him. Having had this intervention, he might have been prepared to forgive the abandonment. At least, to realise the value of taking revenge was negligible. His counsellor would call that growth. However, an outsider might comment this was easy to say, given the eviction or revenge was executed and now could not be undone.

1995

Timmy came here by night. The building was in darkness and locked up for the evening. He would go around the back and into a brightly lit up "prefab." This was a modular building on grounds in the corner of the back car park which was otherwise badly lit up. In it he would attend G.A. meetings, gamblers anonymous to the uninitiated. He often told the newbies how ironic it was he had this problem, giving how he saved a friend from a bad gamble back in their school days.

2020

MJ was skittish a bit whenever the barn was man heavy. Jack's powers of observation were at their peak, so he saw the subtle flinches. Her frozen frame when some delivery guys were roughly dropping off packages by banging them on the floor. That day she seemed particularly nervy. He knew how she felt about men. And why! So, he introduced her that evening to his idea of therapy. If nothing else, it showed he cared.

19:56 in the evening.
Any evening not just with MJ in 2020

Delaney sought counselling; at the times the psycho offices were closed. His shrink was in a bottle. The bar counter was his couch. He was self-medicating. It helped. At least as far as he was concerned.

The night MJ joined in stands out for it was perhaps a herald of new beginnings for the pair of them. MJ was not a drinking prude. She minded not if you did or didn't. But to over imbibe, that was the sin. Drinking too much liquor was how her father had become the monster of some repute.

She explained a bit in fairness, giving the background on what have been a personal and harrowing story. Her Dad had been a worker all her life. He was busy building Ireland until 2008. Global financial crises tend to take the wind out of things. By 2010 what was there for him only state handouts! His dignity hit the floor and he hit her mother. At first, he half apologised, promised better things. Eventually he stopped apologizing and started blaming her for having to do it. MJ couldn't watch it anymore and so didn't hang around. Nor would she remain here if Jack's plan was similar. If JD was to drink himself to paradise, then it would be a foolish one. She would not swap one alcoholic for another, even a nice one like Jack. He needed a new plan.

Jack listened to her, reassured her that all men were not as weak as her dad. It would be okay. And he listened about his own circumstance too, or rather he heard. He was not happy either. So it appeared she was right. It was around this time he hatched from previous drunken pub crawl discussions in his memory the carcass of a plan to retire. A final score! Just needed to find the right mark.

DESTRUCTIVE CREATION
1965

Life in Kimmage had promised to be the land of milk and honey for the Cohen clan. Their house was tidy. A three bedroom with a tiny back yard. As a new build it was quite posh. By that, you can infer that the toilet facilities were actually in the house itself and not accessed via the shed in the back yard. This is what passed for progressive and modern at the time.

The new threesome, Amran, Shira, and the young Aidan settled in nicely. The name Aidan was chosen to help the youngster feel Irish over Jewish. It helped that it was in some way like his Abba's name, Amran.

Those early years were fairly happy for them all. Shira as wife was central to ensuring the boy was loved. He was played with by his mam who used to play funny games and sing lullabies. She nurtured too by feeding him the best she could.

To provide good food, modest clothes, what Maslow's Hierarchy of Needs would have on the bottom of the triangular shaped table, the basics required sacrifice. Just as it did and does in every household there ever was.

That came from Amran who often sacrificed quality time to concentrate on work. And so, one definite sacrifice was that dad, Abba, was not always around for the fun stuff and yes, it's true, Amran was a serious non frivolous type, but this does not mean that he didn't go upstairs when he got home late to peek in at his sleeping 2-year-old achievement. He was a doting dad but just in his own way. This reservation again not exceptional for the time, men then just weren't as touchy feely as they would become.

The bills had to be paid, same as every house. This one had extra. Being Jews, they couldn't do serious work on the Shabbos, from sundown Friday to sundown Saturday. For example, for all winter and autumn months an extra 6d had to be found to pay local children to light fires and gather in fuel to keep them going. It was that or freeze. And that would hardly be good parenting!

The years passed on as they do for everybody. Amran tried to teach his son as he got older lessons of economic importance. He would deny a treat to his son if a chore was not done correctly.

In future years therapists would explore what they called his dad's coldness. The parenting handbooks were constantly being rewritten and now people were demonizing the male stereotype of old.

But that was not what messed Aidan up! That had to be losing them both in the stupid pointless crash. They had been such a huge stability in his life. And then they were gone, because of a simple tire blow out. It was not the imperfect parenting he got from them, but the lack of it, at all, that planted his abandonment issues. His "focus not wallow" mantra allowed him not to deal with but bury the abandonment issues. These issues were not helped by the fact that he had been told honestly by his parents of his first mother. Voluntary or involuntary his abandonment by four parents was very real.

It put him on a path. He couldn't rely on others. They kept leaving. He would have to do this on his own. So, he put into practice some of the lessons his father told him and started to speculate in order to accumulate. If having things was ever a metric, he was going to excel.

This would occupy him in his head just long enough to continue burying the pain. It would also bring about another consequence. He would become abhorrently wealthy. Filthy stinking rich.

THE CHICKEN COMES HOME TO ROOST
2023

The team had to go quiet for a while. They knew Jack was formulating a plan. As he worked out the kinks in his head, he tried to have a normal environment about him. He even encouraged a bit of card playing in the group. He always had them play harmless games like Go Fish. Gin Rummy was about the most serious variant he played. This was the case, in deference to his good friend Timmy's weakness regarding gambling.

Although it has to be said, Jack was completely unaware of the fact that that particular horse was well bolted, and the stable door was properly ajar. Jack, therefore, made his usual attempts to keep Timmy away from his vice. However, Timmy was about to have a visitor to their hide away, that would catch Jack up smartish. The Land Rover pulled up to the guy on the scooter outside. He showed where the debt welcher was hiding. The team of four heavies split up around the perimeter of the building. The team leader opened the back half window and lifted out a red brick then went into the glove box in the front and took out some betting slips from the shop with its logo emblazoned on it. He wrapped the brick with them using the sticky tape. He then spilled out the glove box looking for the permanent marker. He definitely had one but in which storage area. He eventually found it in the lidded box between the front seats just behind the handbrake. He wrote his message. He ran hard as he could at the building throwing the brick as he did so. Whilst he was no cricket bowler, he managed to make the brick smash through the upper window, so job done.

Upstairs, the forced domestic bliss of the impromptu think tank was rudely disturbed. The glass breakage made an unholy racket. Shards flew in all directions, liberally all over Jack who was closest. Sitting with his back to the window in question he now had little glass sculptures, resting in the grey wavy nest of hair on top of his head.

He along with everyone else jumped up with the fright of it. Between that and the pub breakages the glass suppliers of Ireland were doing well off this whole affair. Jack normally made that kind of connection. But not today. He was in shock, mouth open trying to process, he turned instinctively towards the window. What the flip is going on? Outside he saw the Land Rover and the heavies. They weren't hard to spot as they stood proudly by the 4x4 wanting to be seen.

MJ was the one to bend down and pick up the brick. She spoke out the writing on it. "100K or else." Timmy clicked but didn't say at first what was afoot as he wanted to see if he could think of a way out for himself. Jack reached for it saying, "gimme that." As he examined it, he noticed straight away that it was on a betting shop note paper. He lunged at Timmy. "What have you done now?" Timmy went backwards to the opposite wall and would have kept going to escape Jack's pent up wrath had he been able. Pinned to the wall he had no choice but to take Jack's interrogation.

He explained how he couldn't help himself, the lure of the gamble just too strong in him. Jack was raging at him. His traditional style of management was to tell his team off individually. But since this caper had unraveled, Jack had been wanting to give Timmy a damn good rollicking.

Timmy finally confessed what exactly caused the brick through the window. Jack was calming down as he realised there was an easy fix to the issue at hand. He asked Timmy to join him in a bedroom privately. When there he initially berated Timmy into a submissive mood. Then told him what his advice was. It was simple, pay his debt. Do it now. Get rid of the bookie. What Jack didn't tell him was he needed to go to an addiction centre. He'd be sure to tackle that with him at a more convenient time.

But back to the matter at hand. Jack pulled a pillowcase off the nearest pillow to him and left the bedroom. He thrust his surrender flag out the window. When he was sure he had their attention down below he popped his head out after the flag. "The man you want, I'm sending him down! He's going to pay his debt. This ends peacefully."

Heavy type number one nods in the affirmative. Jack retreats inside. "Timmy go down and do what you need to!" He looks away from his colleague towards his femme fetale's still sitting at the cards in shock. "Any chance of finding something to block up the window?" he asked them to stir them to action. He then stayed muttering on as to whether he had to do everything for this crew.

Timmy had grabbed a laptop and was still hearing Jack through the plasterboard lining the staircase. He got slower as he got nearer the door. He did not know what fate awaited him. The bookie involved was known for NOT being very forgiving.

As he opened the door and stepped out to his pursuers and his uncertain future, a still angry Jack had the girls card boarding up the newly ventilated window above them. Whatever happens to Timmy, it was all his own fault! Timmy apologised. Explained how he panicked, but to pay up was no bother. He would even transfer 10% on top to cover the cost of collection. You could hear the nervous delivery from above although the view of same was now hampered by the fact that there's no such thing as transparent cardboard.

Heavy number one took to the phone and repeated the appeal for clemency to his boss man. He listened carefully as the boss man pronounced judgement. All Timmy could hear was the henchman occasionally going "uh ha" back down the phone. A grunt of agreement, a signal of message understood. Timmy still looked worried as he saw a smile appear on the heavies face. He liked what he heard but would Timmy?

Hanging up, he addressed Timmy thus. "The boss wishes to thank you for coming to your senses before things got overly unpleasant." He smiled again.

"However, we can't let this kind of thing go unpunished. It erodes his authority. You did pay extra and so he wants us to just break one finger as opposed to your whole hand." With that, a lesser ranked collection agent grabbed Timmy's arm and was trying to pick a finger. Timmy's face lost all its colour as he tensed up and struggled and resisted.

Upstairs, the noise of the scream was loud. The girls looked upset and fidgeted about the room unsure how to help. Even Tamsin cared now for her co captor's outcome. Jack just assured them it would be over soon. Timmy deserved this and he'd have to take it. Now that Jack had allowed himself to be annoyed with Timmy, it was hard for him to be empathetic.

The Land Rover party and the chap on the scooter decided their work here was done and scrambled back to their vehicles and started engines. A swift withdrawal was always a wise course, lest a concerned citizen calls the police.

Like an embattled knight returning from the crusades to the safety of his castle. It is often said that a man's home is his castle. This romantic view could be how some would describe Timmy as he returned upstairs. Instead of dragging the dead weight of a heavy sword by his side this exhausted and emotionally drained warrior held his bad hand with his good. One finger, his wedding ring finger actually, (except of course he did not have one due to being single) was limp, bent a funny shape and now going the colour of a blackberry.

Jack showing no emotion looked at him and asked, "It's over so?" his pitch raised to signal his question. "Tis," came the painfully enunciated reply. Then Jack's humanity returned. "Looks nasty, eh! MJ will take you to the private injury's clinic in town. Get back soonish, then let's finish this thing!"

THE ONES THAT GOT AWAY BECAUSE OLD HABITS STILL DIE HARD
1981

The Mother Superior had a busy autumnal evening ahead of her. Nellie Madigan was calling in. It had been a few years since she was a client at the convent. She wasn't adjusting very well. She struggled to accept the situation. But what choice did she have?

As the nun braced herself for the difficult night ahead, she sipped her tea from a bone China cup and broke a digestive into communion wafer sized titbits. Eating them slowly as a treat should be enjoyed and savoured.

Nellie when she arrived, was let through the big doors by the number one nun herself, as all in her charge were in evening prayers. They would be retiring soon. Anyway, they did not need to be burdened with the weighty meetings of this evening.

Nellie signed the visitors book making a point of writing in the purpose column, "to get my babies back!" The nun showed her into her study. The usual pointless exchange took place. When even Nellie realised in its futility, she got up and said in a loud voice as exiting the study heading for the main door, that she wished them all dead.

A handful of nuns who met her at different stages of her leaving could later testify to her palpable anger. She also met a man coming in as he was heading for the door. She ploughed through him. He had to give way or be pushed over. Charlie Boswell was the man. He was the son of the founder of Boswell movers a local courier/removals firm. Some fees for the month remained outstanding. His mission again stated in the visitor's book "to settle accounts". He too told of how hurried, frustrated and erratic the poor girl was that evening. The guards noted him to be a dependable young chap, only 20 now and already having had to take the reins of his recently deceased father's business. A solid character.

Nellie was to meet her hubby of seven years now, Tom Delaney. Another chance of happiness, of a hopeful many, was nestled, in-belly-ed if you like, well within her at thirty weeks. So, they needed what was about to happen like a hole in the head.

The oversized blue lights were making their way to Nellie's home farmstead. The sirens were on too suggesting these guards were on urgent business. The station sergeant followed in a brown Cortina.

He jumped out of the car and strode up to the half door. Mrs. Madigan appeared leaning over it like Judy in a Punch and Judy puppet show. "That's the way to do it," the marionette, turned glove puppet, catch phrase. Mrs. M said nothing though. She simply waited for their explanation. "Mrs. Madigan, I wonder is Nellie at home."

"What do you want with her?"

"Is she here Madam?"

"Nellie …..NELLIE ….the police are here. They want to talk……"

By then Nellie, not long back from her walk still in her coat and headscarf, appeared in the half door and started opening it. "Miss, can you come down to the station with us? We have some questions to ask you." She agreed and was bundled into the car. Considering her rotundness and her duckish waddle, the police were physically firm with her. The convoy was now on the return journey, the blue light getting smaller as the Madigan's, who embraced by their front door, looking soulfully at their daughters abduction powerless to stop it. Dad snapped out of it first. He told mam to ring their Solicitor and get him into BallyGortMore station. He jumped into his own motor saying he was going in to see if he could help her. He'd ring with news so stay by the phone.

He was true to his word. Much later that evening he rang home. Nellie was being held on a murder charge. Of whom, she asked? The Mother Superior came the response.

The day or so that went by was very nerve racking on everyone. Nellie was being interrogated vigorously as would be expected in early eighties Ireland. The Archbishop was putting pressure on them to get a result. Not to mention their own big shots at Phoenix Park HQ. The heat was on them. Their solution was to redirect it to their lead suspect.

She was sustaining a barrage of questions. They knew she had been at the convent and to quote: "There's no point in denying it so."

"Ah, why would I? I was there, I saw the creature you call the Mother Superior. Nothing motherly about her. She did think she was Superior to us innocents!"

"You had words."

"We often had words!"

"Why?"

"Because she could have helped me get my children back. But she did nothing."

She then went on to swear she left after a fairly vocal rant. And when she left the nun was very much alive, drinking tea and eating biscuits. The guards kept interrogating her over and over. Tom Delaney paced the lobby with Nell's pater. Both men consoled each other that she was innocent. This madness would end soon.

Her solicitor was by her side. His bill would mean they
would have to sell a few sheep to pay it. Money was not the
worry now. Everyone just wanted to get Nellie home. The
authorities had a working theory, there was a missing metal
bookend on a shelf near the exit door. Someone got cross
with the nun, hit her in the head and scarpered. The nuns
assigned to housekeeping said that when dusting that
afternoon there was two, a pair of bookends. But one was
now missing. Blunt force trauma it was called. More days
passed. Everyone official had decided she had done it. Well
it could only be her or Charlie Boswell who conducted
business with the nuns often. He always carried a brown
cardboard file cover protecting a few outstanding invoices
he needed settling. As it happened Nellie blew past him
with such a pace that the file of loose papers fell from his
hand, scattering a good two yards or so away from him.
Nellie didn't notice so offered no help as she bullishly
waddled to the gates. One passing kindly nun did. In
bending down to retrieve a document she observed it
looked like a blueprint of a warehouse or some industrial
complex. She only saw for a second. She never told the
police until they asked the same question they always do.
You know the one. "Can you tell us anything you
remember NO MATTER HOW SMALL. There's just no

way of knowing how significant it may prove to be," and so she mentioned how the file had more than invoices in it. She was thanked and the information filed but the detectives decided that it was nothing. Nellie was the one they liked for it. Nellie was the one with the known motives. But they had not got enough by way of proof never finding the weapon in deep searches of the Madigan homestead and so she was to be released that day. Her nightmare should have ended there.

But unfortunately for Nellie that was not to be. She was walked through the station in the direction of the public office, where her men were waiting. A very small smile of happiness to her problems end was carried upon her unmade-up face. She screamed. Now her face radiated a look of pain. She doubled over grabbing at the wood paneling to stabilise herself. A crimson-coloured puddle seeped through her skirt and down her leg.

On seeing this, she cried profusely "No, No. Mo Chroi, A Leanbh." The men comforted her. She was rushed to hospital. The doctors did all that was necessary to make her safe in her own health, but they were unable to save the baby.

Nellie often wondered if she was being punished for the past. There was nothing she could do to correct that, but it didn't stop her trying. Jack was a solid step in that direction. She had made sure he came within wedlock. But it seems multiple children were not open to her. Why not? Had she not tried so hard to get her two missing children back to complete her family circle? Attempt after attempt had failed. Now she could try again, being adults they could decide for themselves whether or not to see her. Hopefully they would be receptive. But she had to move on, so as not to be swallowed up by her sadness and guilt. At least she had her husband Tom and young Jack who loved her dearly.

STOCKHOLM SYNDROME WORKS BOTH WAYS
2023

Having rushed to the doctors for Timmy's finger to be set privately so more expense incurred, the guys were all reunited back at the bolt hole again. The team watched Jack giving back the money to Cohen in his promises. Their jaws dropped literally as they visualised their gravy train disappear, evaporating one carriage at a time. Every hour, he said. He hung up.

"Jack, what the flip?" "That's our money, you're giving away," and other expressions similar, vomited from the team in choral unison. Tamsin awaited a lull, and simply mouthed a thank you to Jack. It was a solid sign. She would see her baby again.

Jack urged for silence and explained his reasoning. "Guys, we have never had this happen before, I mean never, in 20 years of scamming. An innocent is being hurt by this. A child, I can't have that on my conscience." Of course, none present wanted a baby to suffer.

He was even less patient with Timmy who he now still blamed for a lot of the cockups saying to him, "well if you had not ...."

Yes, the plight of the innocent was a concern but the money loss none of the team liked either. "About the money," Jack went on to explain, "I remember a story from the Bible. A man thinks about how easy things would be for him if he works hard, builds an extra barn, fills it and enjoys retirement. He executes the plan but dies of a heart attack with the new barn full."

"What are you on about?" Timmy asked, but only because MJ wasn't quick enough to be the mouthpiece. "50 million is more than anyone needs. Loss expenses, at worst rounding up maybe 5 million. I know it's a good bit lower, just for quick math we say 5 million expenses. Say we do this till 12 o'clock tomorrow. 20 hours, 10 million, we still have 35 million. I say we give baby 5 million for helping us. That leaves us still 10 million each. We can disappear then, but our conscience will be clear. No heart attack. Barn almost full."

Tamsin had a visceral reaction. "I don't want money. Just help me get him back." Jack said he intended to. He got Timmy to agree to send Cohen a few more bob every hour. "ANY WAY YOU are in no position to grumble, Tim. With all these mistakes you'll be lucky if there's any money left!"

"Right, let's plan for a way to get baby Dylan back." Tamsin could see in Jack's eye's compassion. The eyes of an ally, not an enemy.

They had plenty of time now thanks to the latest version of the plan. Like any other humans in a socially awkward situation, no one knew too much about how to communicate with each other. She tried again to mention Dylan. He listened politely. She continued. This baby was a climber. She would build cushion mountains for him to play on, in and over.

She talked on about how the dad was not ready for the responsibility of parenthood. He had growing up to do. He was sorry, true, but no matter; it was just her and Dylan left together survivors of a fun but temporary thing. A former relationship!

But Tamsin was a genuinely smart cookie. She knew she had to get Jack on side and that part seemed to be working. Once there she needed to keep him there till he helped get Dylan back. This meant letting him talk too. Jack obliged. He took her back to his childhood eviction. The sadness of it. Then in colour, he shared about each subsequent move. The pain and suffering. The woe that befell his family. He had skin in this game literally. As sorry as he was for Dylan's predicament, Cohen had to pay.

If Jack had went on this tirade, during one of his drinking sessions, he would have had troupes of disciples. They would all be agreeing with him. "Terrible 'tis Jack, your round, yeah. The drinks on Mr. D's tab please barman." Bravely, Tamsin chose a different approach, showing her true grit and character. Although she needed Jack onside, she still called out on his self-pitying attitude, "You had two good parents who put a roof over your head. They fed you. They clothed you. In spite of the eviction, you had it good. So, this Cohen guy, I'm pretty sure that Bible you quoted from earlier says, "Forgive them Lord for they know not what they are doing." She swigged the nerve calming, bravery inducing whiskey. "So, get over yourself.

This revenge thing isn't going to fix the hole in your heart. In fact, it just may open some more."

The unwelcome advice was landing. Jack was reeling a bit. Perhaps Tamsin was right.

THE SHRINKING VIOLET EMERGES FROM A VASE

Mary Jean had her head leaning on that steering wheel. She banged into it with a gentle force, enough to act as a release to her emotions. But not enough to actually hurt herself. Her initial thought fleetingly at least was for the burly baboon of an Australian she had just avoided capture from. But he was not the man she feared, not really. That honour went to her dad. Dear old dad.

Then she time travelled back to her last day at home. This was the day she promised her mother to keep in touch. But fear of contact with the old man again prevented her from ever following through on that. She had told Jack how she wanted to help her but could not again, not after last time.

MJ's mum was doing a fry up. It was a Saturday after all. The dressing gown on her had seen better days. Even the cheapest of replacements would jeopardise the food money allowing this treat. Though haggard from last night's abuse from him she tried a happy and brave front for the sake of her daughter, joking over shapes in the toast. "Shur people are seeing all sorts in the toast nowadays."

When her father joined, he seemed more into his paper which was creased badly by the paper boy. "I told you to sort him out. Useless you …can't even do that."
MJ's mum was embarrassed in front of her. He continued, "I will do it, a hiding he will get, mark my wo…"

Stopping mid-sentence, he looked at the wife, scornfully. "Look at the state of ya, show some pride in yerself, will ya?" He grabbed clumsily at the gown half pulling it open. His wife recoiled and mounted a halfhearted defense about having no money.

"So, it's my fault, is it?" lunging at her as he said it. He put her in a neck lock and was watching her turn blue. CRASH went the vase over his head. He fell to the floor landing face up, looking straight into his daughter's eyes, before he passed out. This was just as well as his stare telling her she absolutely was his next victim. Mum noticed that too.

The two women embraced, mother and daughter grateful both were alive. Mum said MJ had to go before the animal woke up. She appealed to her mother to come with her. The fear paralysed the lady though and she asked her daughter instead to go before the monster awoke. That was the last time she embraced her mam. Every day without exception she regretted not bringing her mam with her.

Sobbing over the steering wheel she wondered, could she save her? She stood up to her dad then and probably could so again, as scary as that was. She also could take on her new nemesis, the Australian. She was a survivor. Time to prove it. She turned on the radio, threw down the visor, exposed a make-up mirror and dried her eyes. She drove on back to the war zone that had become their current theatre of operations. Limerick here she comes.

POST HOLIDAY BLUES

Mr. Simpson woke up beside herself, still sleeping. The kids in the room next door were quiet. This B&B was lovely. They were up late last night out partying on Inishowen peninsula. A Donegal pub had a trad night on for music and Guinness lovers. It was packed out. They even had his family Irish dancing by the end. A siege of Venice he remembered. Why had they danced for the fall of a foreign city? He would have to look it up. Google was great that way, he thought. Siege of Ennis, a place in Clare, in the west. That makes more sense. He would have fun back home explaining this mondegreen to his friends down the pub. That night out came just at the right time as it dissolved the strain felt by the aging Simpsons. Their marriage was now very well established but being too close can cause friction. It did for them. She accused him of hepeating himself, and mansplaining everything. Where was the young love passion felt in those first days when Simpson was served in the café by the beautiful Miss Ryan as she was then? This 2nd generation Irish immigrant swept him away back then. Now he worked hard to bring her round, to rekindle that old romance. He succeeded and the dance night went on to be a great experience for them. They both saw each other through courtship eyes again.

Home, work, the normality of life was looming. Just a couple of days more, then the fun would be over. He was glad to have been able to reconnect with his missus. The holiday had worked its magic. He set the phone radio on.

("This morning, we talk to the Director of Operations of C.A.B. That's Criminal Assets Bureau, to learn of their fascinating work.")

Yes, he was bummed to be finishing his hols, it had been such a blast.

("It's how they caught Capone in America and we in Ireland have copied the idea....... Our inspections yield big rewards for the state in lost revenue. Yesterday's raids on a Limerick businessman, yielding nothing. We apologise for the inconvenience caused.")

"Another doze, before we have to get up," he thought dreamily returning to the land of nod. In the background the news was handed over to the sports announcer.

("There was a shocking upset at Thurles races yesterday in the second on the card. The race leading horse, Childer had a fatal heart attack whilst jumping the last. This meant an intense battle for second became a race to win. A photo finish decided on Snookered's right to retain the title for another year being a convincing winner of the same race last year. An interview with members of the victorious Slim & None syndicate to follow, after these...") Simpson was now snoring loudly.

Cohen woke up around seven o'clock. He had checked a few times during the night before and now he expected to confirm it. A million every two hours, fifteen hours passed so account should be up... yes seven and a half million. For a moment, Cohen felt jubilant on having this win. Then he remembered, this was his own money. He took a bite of toast dipping it in the runny yolk, folded up the paper he was reading. Flicking the kettle, he went out the front door to retrieve the post. He tried to be back in before the boil. It was a little game he played with himself. Even the serious enjoy a game of frivolity from time to time. "Damn, kettle won! Maybe tomorrow..." and he then rang Finley.

"Any news on getting them idiots back?" Finley said they'd gone to ground. They'd not gone home. No vehicle pings on Garda cameras since they had their source request them traced, teatime yesterday. Maybe they were already gone. "Maybe they simply have not been on the roads yet?"

Cohen would not be a doormat again. He was powerless when they put him in those foster homes after the car crash. Even more so as a baby, when put up for adoption. Never again. "Just find them." Hanging up, he put the phone on the table, swished away a crumb of toast off his velvet dressing gown, drank a swig of coffee. Where are you? he thought, as he caught up on the last few days post. None of it interested him, not even the letter circular, from Ancestry. com.

Around the same time Tamsin awoke, her head hurt. Jack had given her a whiskey or two, to calm her agitated nerves. So, when she fell asleep, it was deep. Now awake, she climbed out of the most uncomfortable bed ever. She came into the living area. Where were they? The house was empty. She searched frantically. Yes, definitely empty. She went to the front door to meet Jack walking back towards the house. From the foot path, a taxi pulling away, had MJ and Timmy on board.

"Come now, back inside. I'll explain my plan," said himself, "you'll catch your death, it's freezing." Once inside, Jack made fresh tea and rasher sandwiches for the breakfast. And yes, he had thought about legging it overnight. It was a lot of lolly. Why give it up for someone he hardly knew? The simple answer is he knew enough about her to know she or Dylan did not deserve this. He explained that the guys were more useful to be safely away. Timmy could give I.T. support remotely including moving the money about the place. If Cohen got him then, he'd have the money too. MJ came very close to some Cohen gorilla catching her. She deserved to be free and safe. This was his mess; he had a plan to sort it out once and for all. But he wanted his team safe.

She listened, ate toast, drank tea, and listened. And what she heard was, this guy is alright for an immoral kidnapper. As crazed criminal minds go, he was not the worst of them. Not that she had much experience with men (let alone men of a criminal background) since Dylan's dad left.

At least Jack wasn't abandoning her. "I think we have been here in the one spot too long. We need to move, let's go." His instinct was informed by the fact that he knew Cohen had been to his actual home. Ok it was probably Brutus Goon again, for the man himself. They were there. So maybe by vehicle registrations, with the car and van outside, they might be findable.

They'd use public transport. He'd explain the rest of his plan to her along the way. They chucked all the breakfast delph into the sink. They were down the stairs and out on the footpath in 5 minutes. They walked towards the bus stop up the road. Jack pulled Tamsin by the arm to duck behind some parked cars. He had just noticed a Merc jeep turn in the road. It might not be Cohen, but better look a fool after for overreacting, than be caught with ones pants down metaphorically speaking.

Finley jumped out of the Mercedes. He had his phone to his ear. "Yes boss. Just got here. Their vehicles are here. Looks good. Will ring you back."

Jack and Tamsin moved towards the bus stop. A bus pulled in. They were on board and on the top floor of the double decker. From there, they saw the door kicked in.

REWIND 10 minutes: Cohen, after his breakfast, had dressed for a trip to the golf course. He heard his phone and answered. It was the fellow who ran plates for him. They had located the vehicle's location. He sent his Aussie friend.

Now Finley was giving him a blow-by-blow account of the flat search. Coming down the stairs, he told his boss, still on the phone, that they'd missed them. They were gone! Again.

Desiree's day was a busy one, indeed. Dylan woke up pretty early. Normally she would lie in on a morning after a hard night of pub work.

She got going to the baby's rhythm. He was fed, washed, changed and dressed. Far from feeling tired, she felt energised. Her hubby, Ralphie noticed that too. They planned a morning out with him, maybe a walk in the park.

She would have to check in with work on the status of the search for his parents.

As it happened, before she could call her boss, her doorbell rendered such a call useless. It was one of the traders. He and his associates had been asked, when searching for Delaney had failed, to do a few chores. Fetching back into town, baby Dylan, and Desiree, was one such errand. They were also expected to get rid of Delaney when Finley had finished with him, later. Today's uber is tomorrow's undertaker. Then they would get paid and be free of all lunacy. They would enjoy going back to selling the secondhand clothes. Simplicity. They'd never underrate that again, that's for sure. They too were capable of the same kind of operational cock ups as Jack and the Tipperary crew. Double-booking jobs was possible with them too. "Hurry up, girl. We are running late." They had another job on involving secondhand clothes later today. They explained all to Desiree on the ride into town. The life of an entrepreneur, one must accept the earners where one can.

FAMILY REUNION

The bus took Jack and Tamsin out to the airport in
Shannon. It had come to Jack that Cohen knew they were in
the city. They needed to hide outside somewhere. He also
wanted to get away quickly with the mula when it was
finally safe to leave her. Although he was becoming
conflicted on that subject, leaving her. He had chatted with
her a fair bit over the past day or so. Truth is he felt truly
sorry to have involved her. She didn't deserve any of this.
But now, knowing her more, he realised she was a really
nice person. He must make it right for her. In fact, if their
first meeting had been mutually agreed upon, he could see
a future worth exploring. He imagined a simple steak
dinner, a few glasses of wine for her, maybe a whiskey for
him. He would be charming, a storyteller, and a poet. She
would be as she has been, warm and loving. She clearly
had it tough being a single mum. She looked after little
Dylan, providing him succour and a safe harbour. If things
were different, she could do the same for him. Daydreams!

They arrived at the airport and disembarked from the bus.
Entering the Arrivals Hall on a Saturday was always a

sensory invasion. 'Twas like an ant hill full of movement and the hum of people. They blended in and looked for two seats to base themselves for a while.

He had thought about the next move and felt he needed to talk to Cohen. He rang him on yet another disposable phone. He never went through so many of them on one operation before. Another reason this job would stand out, albeit a trivial one, it had to be said. He rang Cohen. Cohen was in the club house bar. The greying skies had discouraged him from swinging at a few balls. He sat with whiskey in hand, looking out at the braver souls. Their wild swings were visible to him; in the same way an audience member can see the overly dramatic acting at an amdram production.

His phone vibrated in his pocket. It was the money grabber.

"You've been keeping your word. I've got some back, but I want it all back."

"How's the child?" Jack asked. He knew Tamsin would want an update.

"He's being minded. He is ok. Bring me the rest of the money and I'll have him with me to return to his mother."

"Right, I'll come meet you back at the pub. I will have the money with me on mammy Madigan Delaney's life …and daddy Delaney's too. Just have the child. And by the way, we saw you came to visit us. No tricks this time."

Hanging up, he looked up to catch Tamsin's eyes looking deeply on him. She was coming to trust him. He told her he'd go to meet Cohen and bring Dylan back to her.

Cohen paused and processed the events so far. He was clearly upset after the call. The staff assumed he was just annoyed to have not caught them yet. "On your mother Madigan Delaney's life, eh?" he shouted. "We'll see about that."

Jack went back to the front of the airport. Having hailed a taxi, he sat in the back, mustered a breath to give the driver the address and slumped into the seat. As the taxi started to pull out, the back door opened. Tamsin jumped in. "Sorry, I want to come. Got to get my son!" Jack saw that primal

need of motherhood again. He knew better than to
challenge her on the subject. So, they drove on.

"Just be cool, please and do it my way." Jack pleaded. The
taxi took them back to Cohen in Limerick. The journey was
a very quiet one. The nerves were building and the two did
not know how to settle them.

The driver assumed the two a couple and tried to chat as
they do with them. Sport, no response! Politics, silence!
Lover's tiff, bound to be, he guessed.

They parked near the pub; they alighted from the car and
paid the driver. As they faced the pub its doors opened. Out
popped a relieved looking Finley, "G'day." He held the
door to allow entry on the part of the con and his colleague.

He slammed the nuisance into a seat. "Glad we can have
another drink together." Cohen said feeling a tad smug. "It
appears I'm winning again."

"If that makes you happy!" a beaten looking Delaney
chipped back. Cohen genuinely congratulated Delaney, for
almost getting away with everything. Having tired quickly

of the theatrics, he asked Delaney for the tablet back with the codes and Bitcoin.

Delaney pushed back, "Where's the child?" Cohen said he had Desiree minding him out back. "Let the mother go to him." Aidan gestured for one of Finley's boys to bring her through to the back. Then he turned to Jack and asked for the money.

Jack took a tablet out of his briefcase. He handed it over to Aidan. Some of his crew had scarpered already, with their shares. There was still about a third of the loot intact. How to get it was on the tablet. Cohen laughed. He had already ten million back, so this meant he would have back twenty-five million. It was not going to be as bad a day as it might have been and now he was going to have to hurt these people for what was still outstanding. More fun.

"You have been a worthy adversary brother. Now I do have a problem. The child's mother." Cohen paused. Delaney jumped in, "Sorry, what did you say?"

Aidan repeated the phrase, "The mother." No, no, Delaney had heard that bit. Hopefully things would be over before it got that far. "You called me brother. I don't get it." "You really have no idea! Ah come on, I thought you were the clever man who can con anyone. Ahead of everyone. And yet here you are with no idea."

"About what?"

"Wow how truly emotional a day, this is for you! Drum roll needed for this news. Here goes. We are brothers. You and I." Delaney looked confused and Cohen was enjoying the big reveal.

"I know right. I'm just a few hours ahead of you, on the knowledge curve. It's quiet something."

"My birthday was 15/4/63. My mother is Helen Madigan. I believe she went as Nellie. She didn't want me."

"What, how, are you, my brother?" Delaney was genuinely getting upset. This revelation was news to him. Shocking, alarming, stomach churning news. His mind regurgitated the information but was struggling to process same.

"Our mother had a fling with a famous horse man, by the name of Flanagan. It appears I was unwanted, rejected in favour of freedom. Put up for the uncertainty of adoption. My dad told me before he died my real mother was a Madigan. I did my research to find her. It didn't go well. I didn't know her new name was Delaney. It brought me to a chap named Brady from the adoption crowd. After applying a little "pressure" he told me who and where my "mum" was. A week later I got told to evict her, it's a funny old world, no!"

Jack was truly dazed by the news. His mum and dad never told him this. If true, he and Cohen were half-brothers. Why would he evict his own mother? This only heightened the hatred he felt for this particular adversary. He was evil as far as Jack was concerned. He most certainly was going to pay for it.

BUILDING YOUR BRAND
1990

Aidan arrived punctually at the Dermatology clinic. He had taken the day off from financial wheeling and dealing, which he enjoyed, to handle something he finally now had the means to deal with. His face!

He had a bit of time before they would get to him. Best then to be comfortable, he thought, so he ambled over to the gents next to the waiting area. After doing what had to be done, he washed his hands in front of a ginormous mirror, the full length of the wall holding the sinks taking in a panoramic view of himself as he did so. He could see the birthmark. In fact, he was focused on it. It's a truism to say, give people a clean piece of paper and put one dot on it. That's all they can see; they focus on the dot not the white expanse in front of them. People have been like this with him his whole life and quite frankly he was sick of it. What was the point of earning spondulix if he couldn't better himself with it?

Birthmarks like his they told him, if left alone, could cause skin cancer, which after one year could kill him. Then there were the girls. There was always one who enjoyed hanging around with a freak. But most of the nice ones were put off. They just were, no point in dressing it up differently.

Aidan was just a normal young man who wished to be liked the same as everyone else! The rejection of a mother scarred him. The death of his adoptives also pushed the sears deeper. But the trauma of his facial recognition turned that scar into a cattle brand searing his very soul.

From now on it didn't have to be that way. He could have corrective surgery to fix it and as he stared into the mirror memories resurfaced.

1975

Shira was busy preparing for Shabbat later that evening. The house was quiet as she had it to herself. Her hubby was yet to return from work. Aidan had briefly returned from school but had gone out to the football green.

It was an area of grass, the council intended for general play, to be used by dog walkers and joggers in their colored leotards and the like. Mainly though, kids played footy on it. The Sasanach game as some called it, was very popular around here. Because two groups were required to be there to play, visually they were always noticed. Hence the green became known as the football green.

Aidan was amongst a group of youngsters who did not know any better but to ridicule difference. So, his face meant to them, that he was literally a marked man. The odd verbal comment or an overactive tackle from one of the gang, was normal enough.

On this day Aidan found himself heading for goal with the ball at his feet when he became entangled in a stray sports boot lace. Those suckers are long when untied, snake like. All too easy to be tripped up by! One of his opponents poked at him, one of his teammates even quipped how he couldn't see where he was going past this spot on his face. Aidan snapped, jumping on the guy swiftly. "Fight, Fight, Fight," the spontaneous teenage chant could be heard out on the pitch extremities, by a few adult spectators who dutifully broke up the shemozzle.

Shemozzle. A well-used Irish phrase for any fight because of the chaos caused. Had Jack Delaney been there, the chatty man that he was, he would have explained it was Yiddish (an old Jewish dialect). A fact, he would enjoy explaining to the affected Jew, young Aidan Cohen. It would, however, be a few more years before they met for the first time. A serious few before they met for the second time. For Jack himself was just a newborn who had not yet established a social circle to give his opinions to. Or formed those opinions. He was more concerned over his next feed and when mammy was going to change his terry toweling. He had not even got the tan in the pram yet. So, Jack was not yet an annoyance to Aidan. Brother against brother was their future but not their current reality. For one thing Jack was normally only this verbose over a beer. Again, for obvious reasons his shot clog days were not yet realised. Jack had not hazed Aidan. Young master Cohen was being hazed by his peers. That was the current crisis. The solution was only for Aidan to find. So, Aidan simply went home, up to his room and cried.

All he wanted was to be the same as his peers, not noticeably different. His bedroom door slamming, followed by loud sobbing was heard by mammy Shira downstairs who was situating candles in their ready position for the festive day commencement later that evening. Shabbat was about being a family together in worship of God. It was apparent her son needed some family time more urgently. She climbed the stairs to oblige. Once there on the landing she saw his door ajar despite the slam. But only because he was in such a hurry to make to the bed, he failed to push the door fully shut. She leaned on the timber barrier as it creaked its way open. And she walked in. He was still sobbing. Lifting his head up, he called mammy to him. She calmed him and listened carefully as he offloaded his version of the row and how he was fed up with being different.

She genuinely felt for him and mothered him with full on hugs. Shabbat would start soon, and she, he and dad would be together. The world banished outside with all its meanness! Looking forward to the pause in the bullying was a luxury of the time not afforded to future generations due to invasive social media and its effects on our privacy. Bullies are now always nearby. But back then, Aidan knew hostilities were suspended for at least the next day. His mom reminded him of the Jewish value, "Avadim hayinu lepharo bemitzrayim" or, "We are slaves out of Egypt," which comes from Deuteronomy 6:21 reminding Jews they were historically bullied. It was supposed to elicit sympathy for the downtrodden and the victimised and encourage adherents to support them.

Aidan heard her words and got the idea but then applied it to his own life circumstance as follows: mark or not, he would be victimised. It was a call to action from mom to not oppress any! But he focused on his version; be oppressed no more! It would appear his interpretation of the teaching would now set him on a path. Jack the philosopher if there, would take the time over a bar stool and a pint, to debate with whoever, whether it the message or the messenger or the interpretation of it at fault. Once fired up, he'd continue the Jewish had had a bad rap being stereotyped as money merchants when historically they were blocked from most other legitimate enterprise. Blocked by the more dominant to keep them down. Anyway, Aidan was done with being down. Head high from now on.

1990

The door to the gents opened as another patient came in to complete his ablutions. Aidan was jolted back. The mark was part of him, that had made him the tough guy, who was on the up more and more. He'd be OK. The nurse was searching for him in the waiting room as he exited the building happy. He'd wear his brand with pride. It was who he was.

MOVING UPHEAVEL
2023

The local politicos had been in the local papers talking on the subject for weeks now it seemed. In fact, each party took turns getting pictures taken of their man or woman either posed outside the now former county offices or the new modern complex.

The older building was steeped in history and so was becoming a shrine to that, a sort of local interest museum. It was to also have a tourist information hub which would explain to visitors where to spend their money whilst here on their hols. Whilst the two buildings were in their soft launch phase people were encouraged to visit the information office and use it.

The Simpsons did just that. They visited here and found out about places like Cahir Castle.

Some sections had not yet been transferred. Today the removals people were tasked with shifting the paper records out of the adoption's regulators. They were shifting them in the cabinets they had lived in for years and years. Those things weighed a ton.

The boys on the job were contracted removal men from Boswell's. The team leader was none other than the future supremo Darren whose dad had him doing all the grunt work to learn the business from the ground up.

"I tell you, the sooner the government goes proper digital the better!" he grumbled.

"Yeah, it's true a digital file weighs a lot less than a real one," agreed another underling. Yet another interjected without caring for the consequences of talking to the boss sharply. "Stop moaning, get shifting .... we'd be done if your tried maybe second gear."

"Alright, alright. It's not my fault I got a bad back. It's all the years doing this crummy job with yahoos like you."

The riveting banter was interrupted with a papery bang. It came from behind the cabinet being maneouvered onto a sack trolley. Upon investigation it was a big heavy brown case file, dusty and cobwebbed, signifying it had been back there for some considerable amount of time. It said on the cover, which was tightly bound with elastic bands, Helen Madigan. The fellow holding it looked at it for a while trying to figure out what exactly he should do. He noticed the cabinet had an M/N drawer and decided that was the best place for it. So, he opened the drawer and deposited the file. The cabinet was fairly full, so it took a bit of persuasion but eventually swallowed the file whole. To pretend he had never seen it was the simplest solution for him. That file might become a hassle to him if it was found. He would have to mind it, then his HQ may expect him to find someone to give it to. Hassle he didn't need. He just wanted to get to the end of what was proving to be the longest working day he'd had in some time. Darren just wanted to get home, shower, have a beer and maybe a TV dinner and watch the cycling highlights. As he pushed the cabinet to the door he had already forgotten about the file. Who was going to take the Red Jersey? That was now what occupied him.

So, he had no real interest in the file now sandwiched in with the others. It contained the many letters of Nellie. The digitisers would eventually find it and they could do the appropriate thing with those letters. That's what made sense to him as a tired and under paid menial looking forward to a tall one, by the telly.

(Removal men situation means it's Right said Fred by Bernard Cribbins.)

It was a damp September evening. Showered and refreshed, the removal man went to the fridge for a beer. The Vuelta a Espana was just beginning on telly. Let the night begin.

(Again, the film soundtrack, how's about Bicycle Race by Queen. You probably think I'm corny in my choices. Don't forget to post me @nellieskids1.)

All that mattered to Darren then was the cycling and accompanying beverage. As he sipped the beer to the scratchy sound of gear changing necessitated by varying gradients in Spain, he no longer remembered Nellie or her kids.

UNDELIVERED NO MORE
2023

1/4/64
Helen Madigan
Stud Farm Lane
BallyGortMore
Tipperary

Adoptions Regulators
County Offices
Nenagh
Tipperary

Dear Sir / Madam,

I really am at my wits end.

I have been trying now for months to get some traction on deleting this most terrible mistake. These children are mine. My flesh and blood! I have been as vocal as I can be that I wish to have those children back. I come from a good family, and they are willing to support me in what we know to be right. Once they saw what this did to me, they were supportive ever since.

I'm a citizen of Ireland. Don't you work for me too? Why are you so silent? It's wrong, what goes on....

Please help me.
Helen Madigan

A copy of the official reply was also in the file. Presumably Nellie had received its original, many years ago.

15/4/64
Adoptions Regulators
County Offices
Nenagh
Tipperary

Helen Madigan
Stud Farm Lane
BallyGortMore
Tipperary

Dear Ms. Madigan,

Please be advised that we have received
your letter dated April First,1964.
Adoptions are only undertaken when it's
assessed to be in everyone's best
interest. Both were carried out in
accordance with all legal guidances and
parameters.

The Adoptions Regulator will not be able
to take any further action on this
matter.
Respectfully,

BS Brady
Manager In Charge

AS much as I want to help, I have been advised that to
proceed would be most unwise on my part. I respectfully
submit the same to you.

12/8/78
Helen Delaney
Fitzgerald's Row
BallyGortMore
Tipperary

Adoptions Regulators
County Offices
Nenagh
Tipperary

Dear Sir / Madam,

As you will be aware I have been trying to find out how to
contact my children for a long time now. In fact, I have
started a new family of my own. This just makes me aware
I have more kids out there. The twins must be getting older
now themselves. (They are, sur I have their dobs
15/4/63. That makes them 15 years old.) Please at least let
me see, do my now growing up childer want to talk to me?

I have included letters seeking the children's permission to
contact them. Please send them these. I desperately want
to see them to tell them they have a brother now. It would
mean a lot to me.

I thank you for your attention to this matter urgently.
Respectfully,

Helen Delaney

9/10/78
Adoptions Regulators
County Offices
Nenagh
Tipperary

Helen Delaney
Fitzgerald's Row
BallyGortMore
Tipperary.

Dear Mrs. Delaney,

The ARO acknowledge receipt of your most
recent request. The letters will be held
on file until the children involved
reach the age of emancipation, i.e.,
their 18th birthday. At that point it is
expected that we will show the letters
to the children. It will be then at that
point theirs to decide if they agree to
meet you/or communicate in any other
way.

Faithfully,

BS Brady
Manager In Charge

UNPLANNED
1981

Charlie Boswell had taken over the business on the death of his father, the previous year. Most everybody had come out for the funeral. He was well waved off. Many were saddened at his passing. His mam, chief among them. When he went to console her, at the funeral grave side, she put her hand on his cheek. "Ah let me look at you," she said, "Nellie's boy," out loud so even the nuns and the other papists at the back of the congregation in their separate respectful cluster could hear it. "You were more hers, than anyone else's." Most hearing took Mrs. B to be grief stricken and a little incoherent. The Mother Superior understood better. It was a barb at her, public and yet private, almost discreet in its delivery.

The firm was going from strength to strength. An architect was to call by today with the new plans for additional warehousing. Charlie, like all Boswell's, loved machines and so he himself was digging the test holes to ascertain the drainage. He rolled over to the dig zone. He only went down the few feet when he seemed to be banging into some timber. He got out of the cab and scrawled around it by hand. What had he found? As the boxes shapes became apparent, he imagined it was an old paramilitary gun arsenal or perhaps some buried treasure about to make him richer.

Opening the box, he was horrified. The smell was rank. He insta-vomited there and then. He had to throw himself to the ground to get his projectile emitting head away from the box contents. He was grossed out but not stupid. He knew Ireland and its past. He knew who he needed to see next. He covered up the hole again. He rang the convent and told the Mother Superior to expect a visit.

Driving out there in his Beemer, he thought of how this event affected him. They were doing massively well, but any official delays due to the processing of a find would shut him down indefinitely. He had staff and finance outlays to keep on top of. Then there was his fledging family. His recently born son would grow to take it over. So he needed to keep up the momentum. He remembered old war stories that both his father had told him or other people in his presence. His dad was a tough nut. No room for softies in business he would have said.

This train of thought formulating within him was a bit alien to him. But he would do what it takes. He arrived out to the convent and headed into the Mother Superiors drawing room.

He outlined to her what he had found. She didn't attempt to deny they, what he found was, ... care of the convent. She added calmly and with Boswell International. The penny just dropped on Charlie. That was why dad set aside the one percent for the kid's charities. A guilty conscience. There was every chance he would get one too. Perhaps he'd up the contribution to the two percent.

He asked her for hush money from the order. She said they had none. They had given the Boswell's enough of it over the years.

"All in the past now. That practice obviously discontinued decades ago. Best let sleeping dogs lie, eh?"

The Mother Superior looked at her son, eye to eye and pleaded his not doing anything rash. He was a Boswell and wanted it to be a windfall type situation and so persisted.

Dymphna decided that she needed to say more. Perhaps she was just sick of the deception. She explained how close Ivan and her were. How they did this together. Now she was in a confessional mood she blurted out, "You're my son, me and Ivan we......loved each other."

Obviously, that took some processing. Was she mad, did she think him a fool? He wanted cash for silence and that was that. He'd have to move them. That required help. Silent help, the dumbness needed was deafening. That required cash. Otherwise, he would have to get ahead of it and expose it. The nun invaded his personal space. "Please son don't, I beg you."

"Don't call me that!" he shouted at her as he forcefully broke free. "Shut up." She didn't. She kept pushing. She knew it was hard to take it in. She was sorry. She was crying out to him. "Shut up." She didn't. The Mother Superior penguin ice queen was unravelling in front of her son. She was sure proof to any who need it that women are the more emotional half of the species.

Men are stereotypically anger merchants who sort stuff out with their fists. Charlie lived up to this. "I said shut up."

Reaching for the nearby book end he swung it at her. She fell to the floor instantly. A shocked look frozen to her face. Charlie would not be collecting any bonus today. He ran out of the nun's room, seeking the fresh air of outside. Perhaps a bit of air, a pause for breath would allow him to think clearly again.

Outside he fell back against the Convent façade and inhaled large gulps of air. Then came the clear thinking. What had he done? Time to go before she's discovered. Whoever she is…. that nonsense about being his mother. Then he thought better of debating with himself everything there and then. Surely a scarper was in order. And so, he did, his exit actually unseen. Not like his arrival when he ran into that Nellie lunatic. He never thought it and as Nellie never knew of it she could not either. But the nun and Nellie were when all is said so similar. Two demented mothers despite being on opposite sides for so long. It's a universal truth they say, there's more that unites us than divides us. For Nellie and the nun this seemed true. But they would never be able to debate the point together. A nun's rebuttal was never now likely or indeed possible. Such an argument from now on would be one sided. Nellie would go unopposed. Perhaps Charlie would help the police to see that as a motive. Perhaps he could spotlight Nellie. He would certainly try!

FAMILY INTERVENTION
2023

Jack composed himself as soon as he could. It took a good effort on his part as he was still reeling in honesty.

"Ok, full disclosure. I knew who you were. At least I thought I did. That's why I marked you. You are the guy who evicted us. You did that. It really hurt my parents. And now you tell me they were OUR parents. You hurt your own parents. I don't believe that. It's just too cruel."

Cohen reacted. "No. I am not the monster. I told her who I was at the eviction. She said she had tried to find me. Not hard enough, though, eh? I leaned into her that day. Told her I could stop it, just be my mum. I was only a junior at the bank. Perhaps I couldn't have stopped it. But I would have tried. If only she…" He was crying now. She said it was too late. She had tried to reach me a few times apparently. They threatened to commit her if she didn't drop me. So, she did. She had another family now.

Cohen and Delaney were both reliving that moment in flashback. But from their differing perspectives. To both as vivid and as real as it can be. Both upset, disturbed by what memories were flooding back.

"So you torched their lives back then knowing she was your mother." Delaney filled with anger. It was the kind of emotion that fills you in an instant and yet takes an eternity to empty out of you. Cohen really was a bad sort. Maybe some therapist would explain how his actions were explainable considering the rejection. Delaney was not ready to believe that part of the story.

"I think this is a lot of news to take in." Delaney was really shaken. "I need a drink." Aidan had the bar girl out back with the baby. She was a squeamish type, perhaps he would get rid of her too. He would get the drink himself. After all, he would put a bullet in Delaney shortly. A last request honoured would show he's no animal. "What do you want?" as he moved behind the bar. "Rum and Coke, I guess." Cohen made the drink and left it on the bar.

ARRESTING DEVELOPMENTS

Cohen rang the storeroom extension and told his goon to get rid of them all. Now was the time to clean this mess up.

The chap took out his handgun. No one argued when he asked them to go up against the wall. He was just turning to include the barmaid as instructed when a portable gas cylinder, (the type often used to carbonate drinks in a bar) like a small aqua dive tank but just as hard, smacked him. Blamo, he was out for the count. Desiree packed quite a punch. His head would certainly hurt. She needed to hurry. She guided the troop towards the door. She saw Tamsin moving but holding young Dylan firmly in her grip. She was not likely to let him go again, for a fair while. Desiree fleetingly felt jealous. She'd made a good surrogate. Dylan was safe. She leaned on the door release lever. It popped open allowing the natural light to flood in around them as they pushed their way out.

Outside, the noise of sirens was becoming of more audio discomfort, their shriller pitch predicting they were getting closer. Two squads and a paddy wagon were what pulled up directly outside the pub. Four armed-response types jumped out of the van. They burst into the bar, shouting, "Armed police." They cuffed everybody. In an effort to disorientate their prey they were shouting the clichés.

"FREEZE, ARMED POLICE. YOU ARE UNDER ARREST."

The officer who pinched Finley said quietly, so really only he heard it as he was being manhandled, "Let's see how you like it, eh?" The voice was discernable as a newly empowered female, but Finley couldn't place it. He knew he'd heard it before. It just made the moment more confusing.

Then minutes later a plain clothes siren clad car pulled up. Criminal Asset Bureau officers strutted in and started to take over jurisdiction. They could see Cohen was confused. They were waving the tablet at him. Was this the funny money they had been looking for? They would require a chat down at the station. The armed cops steered Jack into the wagon. They would request other vehicles to fetch Cohen back to the station. The Criminal Asset team will be requiring another chat. Where did all this other money come from? He had some explaining to do. The tablet was bagged for evidence. It proved at least 10 million of funny money was in Cohen's possession. The techs would not find any of the rest of it. Timmy made sure of it before he took off.

The Armed Response guys never lingered too long on an oppo. They were happily withdrawing and letting the C.A.B. take over. They pulled out to the van and piled in. As the van pulled out, the whole crew decompressed, from the adrenaline rush of the previous ten minutes. The van was bouncing about on potholed, and speed bumped, manhole covered tarmacadam. The smell of BO in the riot gear was irritating but not overpowering.

They sat heads resting on the vibrating van paneling. They were staring adjacently opposite to one another. A.R.U. person to Tamsin, Dylan, Desiree, and Jack. The van was maybe one or two roads away by now. Jack's frowned face started to turn upside down. Tamsin was relieved for Dylan's safety but now in a panic as to what illegality would she be implicated in. How innocent was she? Maybe at the beginning, all she wanted was Dylan's safe return. But as the ordeal had developed had she not become

Bonnie to Jack's Clyde. "What are you smiling at?" she asked him. In reply, he glanced up towards the people on the A.R.U. side of the van, who started to remove the balaclavas. It was the traders, from earlier in the day. A little view hatch opened from the front cab. MJ and Timmy called in. "We are out and away. We're safe guys! We did it."

The vans cargo now in joyous unison. Everybody in their own way was happy. It was over.

Meanwhile the real police were loading Finley and Cohen into the back of two unmarked cars. The officer loading Finley heard him say he should have stayed at the buildings. He would help with what he knew. They could count on his cooperation. He would rethink on that later, but right now he was a bit panicked. Cohen just wanted to know how they knew to come back. "Who ratted?"

"Anonymous tip," was all they replied. When they pulled back into the local Garda Station, they expected to find the back yard full of the A.R.U. team vehicles. They would have to push through the processing center melee and the chaos. But no one was there. They parked right by the door.

They detained Cohen in his cell. The chat was where was the A.R.U.? They asked the sergeant at the booking in desk about the prisoner Delaney. Where was he? Cohen overheard and now realising he was had, started to shout Delaney was a con man. Nobody at the station was listening. The police personnel were slow to believe they too were had by Delaney. An investigation into him was now inevitable, but at least he had a head start.

GOING, GOING, GONE!
2021

The 9-seater minibus was late to collect its fare as it turned up the gravel driveway of Gleamy house. A full 20 minutes late. The driver was as agitated about this as much as his clients would be. A colleague had promised to fill the fuel tank but didn't, so he was nearly empty and had to detour to refuel. It's really annoying when people you're supposed to be able to trust let you down.

Approaching the main entrance, the seven remaining nuns were all stood by their personal luggage awaiting their chariot. The current Mother Superior was the only one under the age of sixty. Stopping, the driver jumped out and apologised profusely for being so late and explained why, making sure the right person got the blame. Unintentionally further annoying the driver, Mother Superior Edel was not actually too bothered about the tardy arrival and its cause.

She was obviously different from the others in more ways than age. She dressed, yes, in the Orders dark uniform but she went with the less formal slacks, blouse and cardigan. She rarely had to wear penguins gear nowadays.

"It's OK," she said, as it gave the sisters a chance to reminisce over their years in the convent.

Many memories of service, had between them were aired. The place had its sadness, but it did a lot of good too. The nuns recounted how they fed the poor, educated some, and cared pastorally for others, remembering some of the characters they had pass through. They tied together the social fabric not provided at the time by society. The country ill equipped to look after its own. Ireland was the young adult striving to make use of its new independence but finding the responsible side of adulthood boring and difficult. Things like healthcare and education. So rose the religious orders. They were necessary and well-intentioned and that needed to be said. It seemed nowadays, all they ever got was bad press, hence their dwindling vocations. Who in their right mind would now wish to be a nun?

The move was in its final stages, moving the personnel. Boswell's of course had already moved the stuff. All the convent artifacts and private documents had already been delivered to the orders HQ in Dublin. Not as simple as it sounds mid pandemic. Everything was trickier then. Social distancing and other precautions made logistics a difficult job. But Boswell's gave the nuns their usual efficiency. But the Covid was a great distraction. The nuns, priests and brothers along with inept politicians all pushed off the front pages by bat droppings or a chemical weapon of man's making, depending on who you spoke to, or which news outlet informed you.

As the minibus pulled away several of the girls shed a tear for the end of an era. But were as stoic as they could be less a bus full of demented ladies would frighten the driver. His job was to ferry them into Thurles to their new home. A nine-bedroomed bed and breakfast had been bought by the order for €400,000. They would get this back, of course, when the hotel group followed through on buying the convent in BallyGortMore. There are plans to make it a wedding centre of excellence. They would even offer the Chapel as a venue, now of course to any denominations, any couple, who wanted it.

The caretaker would be over later to padlock the front gate and add a sold panel to the Hensbury's auctioneering sign.

He was in the employee of the nuns, but Mr. Hensbury himself had offered him fifty euros to hang the sold sign up, as his own chaps were fitting signs elsewhere. A nixer, the caretaker was very grateful for.

At the gates, to the left coming from the village, was Mary with another walking tour. The nuns who were trapped on board the bus, felt like animals in a zoo exhibit, powerless to stop the peering inquisitive eyes of their spectators from looking them up and down. They knew what Mary did, on that blinking tour. Stirring up bad feelings for them. They imagine that the group was busy judging them for their many supposed indiscretions. Mary would tell them a story alright, and it would be very one-sided. This was to be expected. But there were two sides, and both need to be heard to allow any meaningful healing. The media would facilitate historians for years to come, to try and tell the national story of religious orders, in its correct context, and in fairness to both sides.

The problem with this was, it was a very polarising issue. You were either pro or anti. The middle group, the undecided, unaffected people existed, but by their very nature got ignored. Their position of having no opinion got no airtime so they couldn't be a moderate force for calm in the situation. No one was listening to them.

All that big picture stuff weighed heavy on the nuns now accelerating away to their new home. The problem was this could not, would not be spun by any of them as an optimistic moment. Their new home was already being referred to by them as their retirement home. They were older and they were tired. Some in the group quietly thought how long before the seven, became six then five?

At least this new place gave them warm dry lodgings with a lot less work to be done. Their focus now would be on the spiritual side of life. The new Mother Superior had plans for them to drop the mental disposition of nuns on the run locked in the past.

Some of them were remembering their lost comrades from the convent, the former Mother Superior Dympna for example. Perspective is a subjective thing. Time alters it, no end. Back then the nuns respected their boss but thought that she was a tough woman. Now with the passage of time, it was "poor Dymphna". She was a great boss and a good friend to them. A cruel way to go. As the years had gone by, Mary had even suggested on that excuse of a walking tour that maybe they had done it. The police always thought it was Nellie. But it could have been one of them! They lived with the public's suspicions ever since, so maybe, the retirement home and its anonymity would be welcome. As the driver pulled into the estate in the centre of town, another change for the girls, now committed townies. As Edel tipped the driver, she focused on her plan for them. Sisterly acts of charity and compassion in the community. The rehabilitation starts now.

(I fancy a bit of U2, With Or Without You for the soundtrack here. Please make your suggestion to @nellieskids1.)

TIME TO BREAKUP THE BAND
2023

The family Simpson were exhausted. Their "holliers" were the doing of so much in such a small period of time. It was worth it; they had really connected again. To rephrase that better, they had re-connected. Busy lives swerving from issue to deadline to crisis galore. They all benefited from just being present, valuing each other in ways circumstance can encourage us to forget. This holiday did indeed clarify to them what was important. And yet to ask anyone of them there and then, for utterance of this profound understanding, that they were all subconsciously agreeing to, would simply get a groan, "I'm tired," from her adjacent. "I'm hungry," or "shut up!" from him and her, the prodigies in the rear seats. However, Grandad Simpson was wryly grinning. He knew she was glad to be back "home." She had not lived there since she was three or four and yet as a member of the Diaspora, in a way Ireland would always be home. Making her happy was the best bit for him. Yet if asked, it would be the visit to Cahir Castle, a great day out that was!

The sun's heat switched off instantly, as if a light bulb switch was flicked in the heavens. They had got sufficiently close to the ship, that its shadow chilled them. Without the sun, they felt the windchill. Old windscreen ferry information cards dumped by irresponsible drivers fluttered about the concrete ramps. As they got closer and closer to the ship, the car radio's signal became crackly. ("The Criminal Assets Bureau have said they are making an arrest today following new evidence." Crackle, crackle.) Grandad turned the white noise off. He would be back to his decent music stations on the other side.

Timmy and MJ were hugging at the arrival's hall doors. They were required to go to different ends of departures, one for a European flight. This was MJ. She was looking forward to the South of France. Maybe her school French would help her get a job in a little café in La Cité, the medieval quarter of Carcassonne. Quite the adventure ahead for her, regardless. Especially as she will never actually need to work again.

The other, Timmy, was headed to the USA straight to an exclusive addiction treatment centre. Jack had used a chunk of his change to pay for it. He did not know if Timmy would succeed, but he did know if not, Timmy would blow his fortune, probably on a week in Vegas. He hoped for Timmy to beat it, as they were friends after all.

Jack wished them both well. "It's been quite a ride, eh?" He was sounding as he felt which was quite sentimental. "Yeah, something like that," his team wistfully replied. He got in on the hugging. He turned as they did. It was like a RED DEVIL display as they all moved away from each other without looking back. Actually of course, they all took sneaky peaks back, all not wanting to be caught in the act.

As Jack glanced at Timmy he saw the bright white splint cover on his healing finger. Timmy had put himself in harm's way for Jack more than once. He was a good friend and that's how Jack would remember him.

For MJ too, he had nothing but good thoughts. He had been her protector for a while now. Still, he was so proud of her. She seemed to be growing bigger than her fears. She seemed ready to live again. He would miss her like a dad, as corny as that sounds.

The friends had memories which were popping into their heads as they were realising that this was it. The end was nigh. This prompted anticipation of what was next! MJ got a land when she found out almost immediately as she approached her gate to see her mam waiting in the seat nearest the gate. Mam jumped up as she approached. It was a loud happy reunion. Jack had done it again. "I missed you," they said to one another, babbling over each other in their excitement.

Jacks flight path in pulling out of the group hug took him straight into the arms of Tamsin with a buggy full of a very happy, that is to say an emotionally scar free, baby Dylan. Jack said, "Right let's get you a passport." Tamsin replied, "Then maybe a beach holiday, eh Dylan?" As she spoke, she played with the babs in the buggy. Jack interjected playfully, "Too much sun is bad for babies, what kind of mother are you?" Now he was just laughing at her.

RIGHT TO REMAIN SILENT

The Guards were processing the chaps as fast as they could. The holding cell had a few within, two of whom Finlay and Cohen stoically were quiet. Sitting looking into each other's eyes, they knew not to say too much. Cohen was eager to rat out Jack. If he could not have the mula, neither would Jack. He would be incarcerated the same as Aidan.

Finley was assessing if Cohen was in a snitchy mood how much trouble would he put Finley in? Andrew dismissed it though, as a merited thought. He did this because he was just the muscle, the hired help. Surely the financial scale of Cohen's misappropriations would make him the one the Guards would want brought down. He could make a deal. He wondered if Ireland had a witness protection thing with Australia. He could just go home. He kept looking at Cohen.

He remembered why Aidan hired him. Master Cohen had been to a night spot of note in Dublin. He'd had a little too much of all the vices, so definitely not practicing the restraint of his religious forebears. On the footpath outside an opportunist had at him thinking of the rich pickings that would surely come his way. Andrew Finley off duty from some building site and on the town, himself put the opportunist in A & E regretting his life choices.

He then helped Cohen home. Cohen, seeing he could handle himself, hired him as a minder. He paid well and asked Andrew of nothing but loyalty. Anybody who didn't show Cohen that loyalty was normally dealt with by Finley for Cohen. There came to be a shared investment of effort in the project of growing the empire by the two together. Could he drop all that and abandon his boss to the fate of a has-been? He was still contemplating that when Cohen was fetched for a quick chat with his lawyer.

In the separate interview room, the two men strategised. Finley looked through the cage bars and saw the legal guy leaving the room in a sheepskin and smart suit. It can't be …is it? He thought it was Jack, but it was far enough away. He could be. He must be mistaken.

Cohen later that night recanted all the drivel about the Jack character. He was desperate and in shock and would have said anything to spread the blame away from him. But now he had calmed and said he was exercising his right to be silent. He would cooperate no more.

For Finley was right. It was Jack who played the part of the Cohen legal team. During a quick exchange he pointed out that he knew Cohen had more dirty money stashed somewhere else. A man as clever as he, had to. So, Jack was not offering money for silence because that would be bringing coal to Newcastle. His proposal was much more interesting. He would have his back on the outside as a brother should. He wouldn't abandon him in his hour of need. It was like Cohen's abandonment issues were dissolving away. His blood was once again offering a safe harbour. A sense of tangible identity, of belonging, could be his once more. Nellie's kids would be a kind of family, at last. All he had to do was remain silent. Cohen thanked him for this gesture even though he knew Delaney was trying to save his own skin. Aidan couldn't help it, even mentioning how he missed having a family since his parents' crash. They were buried in Dolphins Barn cemetery. Quite handy was this Jewish burial site in relation to his family home in Kimmage. And yet he found himself wishing he had been a better son and visited the grave more! Jack promised him he was now family. The price, not thirty silver pieces, just his silence.

DESIREE'S DESIRE
2024

Hubby Ralph put the bin out. It was one of the little ways he could help. Desiree will be busy today. She had two youngsters in the kitchen. Once fed they would need to drive to school. Ralph would volunteer to help with that too. The social worker had said he would be dropping over a baby, just till the end of week. They needed time to see if the parents could work things out. Maybe with help, they can create a more stable environment for the baby. If not a more permanent solution would be applied. Desiree was just the foster mum.

Ralph looked on at how she juggled so many challenges and thrived on it. Desiree was just so maternal. She was so good at it, she enjoyed it. He was so happy for her.
But it wouldn't have happened without the windfall. They upgraded to a six-bed detached in the suburbs. Half the rooms had ensuites for the older kids. The garden had a great deck for teenage hang out activity and a jungle gym that took a team of three, two days to put up.

Desiree was able to buy quickly and without fuss as a cash buyer. If she ever wanted to sell, she would, and quickly too. This was a great location. Even without the help the 2023 recession and property bubble bursting meant she had got it cheap. She was savvy and would only sell if it was ever highly valued again.   But none of that mattered to her right now. For her, it was about giving these kids a chance. A sense of place till they found their own. She knew and said often, "We just all need to belong."

A HISTORY LESSON
2024

It had been a nice few years, since the goings on in BallyGortMore. Mary stood outside the shop. This was the first stop on the walking tour. She advised the group that they would be wise to buy a water and maybe a choccy bar.

Tamsin, Dylan and Jack had returned from their holidays. Aidan Cohen was a crook but not a snitch, so he had told no one of authority of his brother's part in anything. That's not true of course. He told the Gardai that Jack was a con man just as slimy as him. But before he could say anymore, he had a visit from his legal counsel. He was a lot less vocal after that call, even serene. He recanted everything he had said about Delaney. So having established it safe to do so Jack and Tamsin just kept running Deals the warehouse legitimately. It was time to stop the scamming so as to ensure there was no more local interest in him from the law. Anyway, retirement from that life was supposed to happen after the scam of the century. It was what he wanted.

Catching up with emails, Jack sat in front of the screen pensively. As Tamsin brought him a fresh cuppa, she asked, "Why so gloomy?" He explained that the ancestry website had just alerted him to having a possible murderer in the family. It click-baited him in. Now he was looking at newspaper articles suggesting his mum a suspect of the nun's demise. This made him sad to think of his dear old mum this way. So, the three closed up early. They popped by a florist and bought some beautiful lilies. They then drove out to the cemetery and laid the flowers by his parents' grave.

Jack told his not present mother how he had found out on the internet that a visitor's log existed for that night. This Boswell chap, it had to be him. As Nellie was never actually charged, perhaps Jack would let sleeping dogs lie. After all, he knew his mum would never do what they accused her of. That was enough for him. After a session of fond remembrance, in the form of a one-sided dialogue exchange with his interred, he rose and quipped as they walked away, "Ye wouldn't believe where I'm going next." Back in the car with them. The trip to Dublin took no length via the motorway. At Dolphins barn, they searched with the help of a warden of the cemetery for the Cohen plot. They solemnly in spite of not knowing the people paid their respects. Positioning a small rock the size of a fresh scone on the headstone, Jack said out loud this was on Aidan's behalf. He apologised if he got it wrong, but the internet suggested it was the appropriate memorial.

Meanwhile now safely back in routine in Sleepsville in the English Countryside (on the sunny southeast) the family Simpson had shared an enjoyable breakfast together. Croissant and coffee for him and a hard-boiled egg with three well-appointed soldiers of toast in accompaniment for her. Scrumptious!

Now he had gone, work wards. In leaving they had joked about how in a few more years (2¾ actually) he would retire from office labour and then every day would be as it was in the emerald isle, fun times ahead!

She put the kettle on again. She liked to race with it. Its aim to boil, hers to retrieve the post, so she can read it with a fresh cup. Out she bumbled in dressing gown and fluffy slippers. She opened the American reproduction letterbox. The type with the little flag by its door if full. She liked it, the ritual. Enroute, she saluted a neighbour bringing in his bin. Once inside, the kettle was only coming to the boil. She would have a nice brew as she read the envelopes. One was from the Government Adoptions Regulator.

Her parents had told her she was adopted a long time ago. In fact, they never hid it from her. She at first did nothing with this information. But in late nineties or was it early noughties, she realised any relatives were ageing too and tried to make contact through the proper channels. Nothing came of it and life was busy for her with her real family. She just kind of let it drop, not intentionally, it just happened. And now they were writing to her. As she read that fateful letter, she fell into her chair crying uncontrollably. They had found her Irish or natural mother. Problem was, she was now deceased.

But this was only the cover letter, inside was another. This one from her mother seeking to make contact. It was fourteen years old, signed "Your mammy Nellie, Ne xx."

(Maybe here would be a good place for The Saw Doctors song How I feel About You Now. Again, gimme yours.)

23/5/10
Nellie Delaney
BallyGortMore
Tipperary

Margaret Simpson
C/O Adoptions Regulators,
County Offices,
Nenagh,
Co. Tipperary.

My dearest Margaret,

You need to know that I have tried to find you for many years & wrote lots of letters in this regard. Please let me explain meself. You deserve that!

As well as a deeply religious place the Ireland of your birth was a very poor place. It was not like now. Sur they, the government give handouts for everything now. Back then it may as well have been the third world. Even if you could endure the stigma of unmarried motherhood, could you feed the extra mouths?

I don't want to sound callous now, but I mustn't mince my words either. You deserve truth, mo chailín! The circumstances of your making were not pleasant for me. I was abused. If you wish to meet up, I will tell you more about your father but only if you want me to, ...such painful memories. I'm tearing up just telling you this much.

You must not feel unwanted. I admit I was confused at first, perhaps even relieved to be unburdened of you. But only days after I knew I had made a mistake in giving you up. (Sorry more tears than ink on the page now.) I tried time & time again to find you both but to no avail. At one time in the past your brother was made known to me, but at that time I wasn't emotionally ready for a relationship with him. I've regretted that decision ever since, and so took up my search again. Please forgive me.

Mammy

Ps I realise I should ask is it ok to call myself that. I haven't exactly been there to earn that title. I mean no disrespect to the lady who raised you, Your Mammy. I suppose it's a big thing to ask but can you make room for another mummy?

Nellie Ne xx

The postman a vital part of any community was busy that day in Limerick. He popped a letter into Aidan Cohen's American Letter Box. It was A4 size and so needed folding to be insert ready. It was a letter Cohen could not read from his prison cell. It's also true that he already knew what it was telling him. But it appeared that officialdom was catching up with the jungle drums of Ireland. It was from the Adoptions Regulator.

Raghnall Cagney

26/11/24
Adoptions Regulators
County Offices
Nenagh
Tipperary

Aidan Cohen
27, The Dell
Limerick

Dear Mr. Cohen,

We are writing to you with some important news to
impart. You are in fact adopted. Your natural mother
wished to contact you earlier, but this letter was
misplaced. She has since deceased.

Please contact our office during business hours and
we can give you the necessary information so you can
make an informed decision on how to proceed.

In Anticipation of your reply,

BS Brady
Manager in charge

That morning Darren Boswell cycled into work motivated
by the thrilling time trial he had seen on the telly, the night
before. It wasn't raining and if he was honest, he didn't like
using his car since it was borrowed from the Limerick pub
he was lunching in last week. The guards hadn't even
valeted it. Someone had been sick in it. It was hoovered but
the stain and smell remained. R32 or not, it still wreaked.
He would get the lorry valets at it before he drove in
comfort again. On arriving at work, he flung the bike
against the wall and went in the office entrance. The door
was held open by a metal door stop as it had been for many
mornings. It was covered in dust and not very noticeable at
all. A keen eye would note it wasn't a doorstop but a
bookend. But why would it be looked at? It was just
recycled bric-a-brac.

He went straight for the coffee machine. His dad would
emerge with the day's dispatches list shortly. Make the best
of the peace he thought. He looked out a window to behind
the new warehouse at the wild garden, vibrant and yet
serene looking. The architects really wanted his dad to
build the warehouse out further. He steadfastly refused
saying we need to remember where we came from.
Everyone took him to be tilting his cap to the agricultural

bent in the area. Hence the preserved green space. "One of dad's better ideas," he thought totally unaware of the garden's true purpose.

When the tourists came back out from the village's centre of commerce, the guide would hear the quaint little jingle of the shop doorbell. This would be her cue to tell the first chapter of the story, to go back to when it all began, the popular shop assistant who worked in this very shop, fadó, fadó. This would take her the day to do, involve a pub lunch at the hotel which was formerly the monastery so central to her tale. A good bit of craic with the punters would be had. Mary truly loved that part.

Most tourists even the diasporan second gens, liked to think of Ireland as aran sweatered fishermen, cailíní deas, saints, and scholars, not to mention stout drinking romantics. Poteen pickled, quiet men a la John Wayne. They all knew of the spiritual side of the place but trivialised that to after life stories of Banshees and suchlike. This tale showed the national spirituality had a dark underbelly, a sinister sadness.

Yes, it was a job Mary loved to do, to expose that perspective on Irish life. She was privileged to be telling a great story, full of tragedy, romance, history, and drama. Mary had skin in the game. Her mam, her real mam Trish met her, reunited with her, and told her of Nellie, herself and the other girls and their babies. She was very much part of the story. And it didn't hurt for Mary that the tips from the tours were generally very good too.

(To end on a note of optimism the film soundtrack here should go out with John Spillane's The Best Is Yet To Come. Final appeal. Post me your soundtrack for book or film to @nellieskids1. You can also leave any other comments on book, please stay positive though!)

Thank you for reading Nellie's Kids. I'm really very grateful.

USEFUL INFORMATION

Should you find yourself affected by any issues raised in
the book please contact one of the following as appropriate.

Mental Health / Suicide   The Samaritans 116 123
                                          or text Hello to 50808

Rape Crisis Helpline   1800 778888

The Miscarriage Association of Ireland   086-8684103

A Little Lifetime Foundation   01-8829030

Gamblers Anonymous   01- 8721133 or 087-7485878

One in Four   01- 6624070

Find Changing Faces on the internet for support and respect
if have a visible difference.

EPILOGUE

(Now I'm finished Nellie's Kids, I'm wondering N.K.2 would be like.......)

The gray reinforced steel doors opened with a reassuring squeal. A man in a navy uniform gestured for Jack and his unrelated and unattached companions through. As he reclosed it, he said a colleague would be round to ensure they had no contraband on them. Following a brief but thorough search they were ushered into the visiting room. They all were highly efficient at finding their visitee. Most people sat in same places on every visit. Only Jack struggled as it was his first time.

As Jack scanned the room, Aidan realised that he was struggling to find him and stood up helpfully. The guards were a bit spooked by this but not unduly so. Cohen needed unruly types to heavy for him. He was capable of an outburst but nothing the baton wearing guards could not handle. Any way these days he wasn't at his best.

Clocking him, Jack crossed the room and sat opposite him. "Hello brother! I was not sure you would come." He barely finished that statement when an involuntary coughing attack upset his head scarf that had been hiding his involuntarily bald head. Jack charitably chatted in reply, "Cancer getting worse I see."

"Yes, I won't see fresh air again. It's for that reason I've asked you here. I need you to do something for me."

"Whatever it is …forget it. You are as you well know not a brother I'm bothered about." He started for the door.

"So much for our Pax Romano. Am I abandoned again? Don't make me shout out across the room why it's really me in here. You owe me."

Jack swiveled and sat. "Alright, alright, calm down….no need to get excited or make threats or anything. Let's chill, you got five minutes then, sorry ….you are right. You are doing your bit for me. What….is it you want me to do,… for you?"

(If N.K.2 started this way what would Cohen ask next? Your suggestions to @nellieskids1.)

Final dream of film…it must have both Pat Shortt (as Jack) and Keri Condon (as MJ or Tamsin or Desiree) in it. Shop local after all. Up Thurles. I'd love Pierce Brosnan (as Aidan) and David Pearce (as Timmy.) Bring it on!

Final dream of film…at this stage we would be in closing credits. As is done often now, a little clip from the movie should be included. MJ's dad returns home to his now empty house a happy drunk, expecting to find his wife. Her absence angers him quickly. Shouting out to her he crashes about the place destructively until he falls asleep. We know it's him as he knocks over family photos of him, mum and MJ in happier times.

Thanks Again for Reading!

.

Printed in Great Britain
by Amazon

28740852R00165